Also by Sheila Fitzpatrick

The Russian Revolution (1982)

*Stalin's Peasants: Resistance and Survival in the
 Russian Village after Collectivization* (1994)

*Everyday Stalinism: Ordinary Life in Extraordinary Times: Soviet
 Russia in the 1930s* (1999)

*Tear off the Masks! Identity and Imposture in Twentieth-Century
 Russia* (2005)

*On Stalin's Team: The Years of Living Dangerously
 in Soviet Politics* (2015)

*White Russians, Red Peril: A Cold War History of Migration to
 Australia* (2021)

Other titles in the Shortest History Series

The Shortest History of Europe by John Hirst

The Shortest History of Germany by James Hawes

The Shortest History of England by James Hawes

The Shortest History of War by Gwynne Dyer

The Shortest History of China by Linda Jaivin

The Shortest History of Greece by James Heneage

The Shortest History of Democracy by John Keane

THE
SHORTEST
HISTORY
of
THE SOVIET
UNION

Sheila Fitzpatrick

First published in Great Britain in 2022 by
Old Street Publishing Ltd
Notaries House, Exeter EX1 1AJ

www.oldstreetpublishing.co.uk

ISBN 978-1-913083-15-1
Ebook ISBN 978-1-913083-16-8

Text design by Dennis Grauel

10 9 8 7 6 5 4 3

A CIP catalogue record for this title is available from
the British Library.

Printed and bound in Great Britain.

In memory of three Sovietologists from my American life who died while this book was being written:
Jerry F. Hough (1935–2020)
Stephen F. Cohen (1938–2020)
Seweryn Bialer (1926–2020)

and of my Moscow mentor, the Old Bolshevik from whom I learned the black comedy of Soviet history:
Igor Aleksandrovich Sats (1903–1980)

Contents

Introduction

1980 should have been a good year for the Soviet Union. Finally, fifty-eight years after the creation of the Soviet Union and entering the sixteenth year of Leonid Brezhnev's boring but stable leadership, the country could relax and feel that the worst was behind it. Domestically, normality had been achieved; better times must lie ahead. Internationally, the country had become a superpower after World War II, admittedly still number two to the United States, but now at last reaching military parity.

It had been a bumpy ride – a revolution and civil war to start off with, famine in 1921 and revolutionary leader Vladimir Lenin's early death in 1924. Then came a new upheaval, launched at the end of the 1920s by Lenin's successor, Joseph Stalin, involving forced-pace industrialisation and collectivisation of peasant agriculture, with famine in 1932–1933 as the aftermath. The extraordinary bloodshed of the Great Purges in 1937–1938 came next, hitting Communist elites particularly hard, followed quickly by World War II, when the erstwhile pariah state became an ally of the West. With the war's end and hard-won victory came the Soviet Union's unexpected, sudden rise to superpower status in a context of Cold War with the West. Nikita Khrushchev, emerging as top man after Stalin's death in 1953, was a pursuer of 'hare-brained schemes' who seemed to bring the nation to the verge of war again in the Cuban missile crisis of 1962 before he was toppled in 1964.

And then, finally, Leonid Brezhnev took the helm, the stolid, genial man who didn't rock the boat but directed it into calmer seas, understanding the aspiration of Soviet citizens for a lifestyle closer to that of the United States and Western Europe. Brezhnev's task was made easier by an unexpected bonus: as of 1980, the world price of oil (of which the Soviet Union had become a major producer and exporter in recent decades) had doubled since the mid-1970s and stood at an all-time high.

Lenin's cause triumphs, with defeated enemies at his feet, in this 1980 cartoon by A. Lemeshenko and I. Semenova.

Khrushchev had rashly promised that the country would achieve full communism by 1980. The more cautious Brezhnev shelved this in favour of 'developed socialism', an anodyne formulation that stood, in effect, for the economic and political system that already existed in the Soviet Union. But that was fine by the majority of Soviet citizens. They wanted more consumer goods for themselves, not communally shared goods, as would be delivered under the Communist model. It was a post-revolutionary moment, with the Revolution firmly consigned to history. The generation that had fought for it was now dead or pensioned off, and even the cohort (including Brezhnev) that rose as its beneficiaries under Stalin was approaching retirement. Brezhnev's own values in later life were more aligned with those the revolutionaries used to call 'bourgeois' than those his predecessors had espoused. (A joke widely circulated at the time had Brezhnev's mother asking anxiously about his personal collection of expensive Western cars: 'But Lenya, what if the Bolsheviks come back?')

Living standards were up; a previously acute housing shortage had been ameliorated; no national or social groups were threatening revolt. The 1977 Constitution, affirming the success of the building of socialism in the Soviet Union, claimed that 'a new historical community of people, the Soviet people,' had come into being. To be sure, the Soviet Union still had problems: a slowing economy; an unwieldy bureaucracy showing little desire or capacity for reform; periodic outbursts of discontent with Soviet tutelage in Eastern Europe; difficulties with the United States and 'détente'; and in the Soviet Union itself, the emergence of a small 'dissident' movement with little support in the wider population but close ties with Western journalists. After Soviet troops went into Afghanistan on 24 December 1979, an international boycott campaign tarnished the Summer Olympics that proudly opened in Moscow in July 1980.

The West had made a totalitarian bogeyman out of the Soviet Union during the Cold War, equating Communism with Nazism as the antithesis of Western democracy, and one of the tenets of this theory was that a totalitarian regime, once in place, was immutable and could be overthrown only by external force. But that idea seemed less plausible when, after Stalin's death, the regime not only failed to collapse but also showed itself capable of radical change. By 1980, 'totalitarianism', although remaining a powerful and emotive image for the Western public, had lost its appeal for scholars, American political scientists Stephen F. Cohen and Jerry Hough being among its challengers. Even in conservative quarters, hopes that had been cherished for more than sixty years about the imminent collapse of the Soviet regime were being quietly abandoned.

Summing up the consensus at a conference of mainstream American Sovietologists, Robert Byrnes noted that 'all of us agree that there is no likelihood whatsoever that the Soviet Union will become a political democracy *or that it will collapse in the foreseeable future*' (my emphasis). An important text of US Sovietology, published by political scientist Seweryn Bialer in 1980, argued that it was time for the United States to give up vain hopes of regime change and accept that the Soviet Union was there to stay. In a similar spirit, the Library of Congress in

Washington, DC, finally decided – after decades of ignoring the existence of the Soviet Union in response to émigré and Cold War pressure – to bite the bullet and give the Soviet Union its own entry in the library's card catalogue. This was an eminently reasonable move and, as virtually everyone in the Soviet research community agreed, long overdue. But in practice the library might have saved itself the trouble. Within a decade, as it turned out, there would be no Soviet Union to catalogue.

SHORTEST HISTORY (1924–1991)

When I first encountered the Soviet Union as a graduate student, just before the fiftieth anniversary of the October Revolution, I would not have expected to have been one of the scholars writing its obituary on what would have been its hundredth birthday. Its life span turned out to fall short of the statutory seventy – just a few years longer than the life expectancy of Soviet citizens born at the end of the Soviet era (sixty-seven), which was almost twice the life expectancy of those born at its beginning.

Historians' narratives tend, by their nature, to make events seem inevitable. The better the explanation, the more the reader is made to feel that there could have been no other outcome. But this is not my intention with this *Shortest History*. My view is that there are as few inevitabilities in human history as there are in the individual lives that compose it. Things could always have turned out differently but for accidental encounters and global cataclysms, deaths, divorces and pandemics. In the Soviet case, to be sure, we are dealing with revolutionaries who, following Marx, thought they had history taped and knew, in broad outline, what to expect at any given historical stage. 'Accidentally' (*sluchaino*) and 'spontaneously' (*stikhiino*) were always pejorative terms in Soviet usage, denoting things that, according to the Plan, were not supposed to happen; they were also among the commonest words in the Soviet lexicon. These same Marxist revolutionaries, dedicated to the notion of subordinating the natural and economic environment to human planning, came to power in October 1917 to their own surprise and, in defiance of their theoretical analysis of the situation, almost accidentally.

Ironies abound in the Soviet history I am about to tell, and surely this is partly a result of the revolutionaries' conviction that in Marxism they had a universal decoding tool. It told them, for example, that societies were divided into antagonistic classes, each with their own political representatives, and that their party – initially the Bolshevik faction of the Russian Social Democratic Labour Party, and from 1918 the Communist Party – represented the proletariat. This was sometimes accurate and sometimes not, depending on the circumstances, but in any case it became increasingly irrelevant: after the party took power, it soon became clear that the party's main function vis-a-vis the workers and peasants who supported them was to offer the opportunity for upward mobility (a process not recognised in Marxist theory).

Theory told the Bolsheviks that the new multinational Soviet state was a totally different animal from the old multinational Russian Empire, despite the substantial coincidence of their borders, and that its centre could not practise imperialist exploitation of its peripheries because, by definition, imperialism was 'the highest stage of capitalism' and completely alien to socialism. As we shall see, this was a more reasonable proposition, particularly in the early decades, than it might seem at first glance; on the other hand, it's not hard to see why people in non-Slavic regions on the periphery could sometimes feel that being under the eye of Soviet Moscow was not totally unlike being under the eye of tsarist St Petersburg.

The Western view of the Soviet system as 'totalitarian' was not meant to be flattering. But actually, from the Soviet standpoint, it could almost be seen as a compliment, being a mirror image of the Communist Party's own self-image as the all-knowing leader, setting a steady course on the basis of science and planning, with everything down to the last detail under control. The many 'accidental' changes of course and 'spontaneous' diversions along the way were simply irrelevant to this grand scheme, although they will play a large part in my *Shortest History*. They were not irrelevant to the life of people living in the Soviet Union, of course, and the gap between official rhetoric and lived experience was the stuff of the distinctively Soviet genre of political jokes (*anekdoty*) that bubbled under the surface as a constant, irreverent commentary. The contrast between 'in principle' (a stock Soviet phrase provoking immediate distrust, like 'frankly' in the West) and 'in practice' was one of the staples of the Soviet *anekdot*. Another was the Marxist concept of dialectics, which held that socio-economic phenomena, such as capitalism, contained within themselves their own opposites (socialism, in the case of capitalism). *Dialetika*, a foreign word, was a philosophical concept adopted from Hegel, but the prevalence of mandatory 'political literacy' classes meant that most Soviet citizens were familiar with its remarkable capacity to explain away apparent contradictions. The quintessential Soviet dialectical joke was this antiphonal formulation:

> (*Question*) What is the difference between capitalism and socialism?

> (*Answer*) Capitalism is the exploitation of man by man, and socialism is its replacement by its opposite.

The Marxist prediction that capitalism would ultimately collapse and be replaced by socialism (Khrushchev's tactless 'We will bury you!') had been a comfort to Soviet Communists as they struggled against Russia's historical 'backwardness' to make a modern, industrialised, urbanised society. They made it, more or less, by the beginning of the 1980s. Soviet power and status was recognised throughout the world. 'Soviet man' became a recognisable animal, with close relatives in the Soviet bloc in Eastern Europe, more problematic relatives in China and North Korea, and admirers in the Third World.

Then, in one of the most spectacular unpredicted 'accidents' of modern history, it was Soviet 'socialism' that collapsed, giving way to what the Russians called the 'wild capitalism' of the 1990s. An array of fifteen new successor states, including the Russian Federation, emerged blinking into the light of freedom – all, including the Russians, loudly complaining that in the old days of the Soviet Union they had been victims of exploitation. *What Was Socialism, and What Comes Next?* was the apt title of American anthropologist Katherine Verdery's commentary on the post-Soviet moment,

'Sixty Years and It Still Hurts' is the title cartoon by E. Gurov for the Day of the Red Army (23 February 1978). It shows an English lord still smarting at the failure of British intervention in the Russian civil war.

pointing to the fact that in the former Soviet bloc it was not only the future that had suddenly become unknowable but also the past. 'What comes next?' is a question no prudent historian ever tries to answer. As for 'What was socialism?', that can be addressed by political philosophers with reference to canonical texts, but I will take a different tack – that of the historical anthropologist. Whatever socialism might mean *in principle*, something that in the 1980s earned the clumsy name of 'really existing socialism' emerged *in practice* in the Soviet Union. This is its story, from birth to death.

1

MAKING THE UNION

THE RUSSIAN REVOLUTION WAS MEANT to spark off revolution throughout Europe. But that plan didn't work, and what was left was a revolutionary state in Russia – the Russian Soviet Federal Socialist Republic (RSFSR), with Moscow its capital. But there had been upheavals with a variety of outcomes in non-Russian regions of the Russian Empire too. The Baltic provinces chose independence; the Polish provinces opted to enter a newly created Polish state. But by the end of the civil war set off by the October Revolution, other regions had established their own soviet republics, often with a little help from the new revolutionary state's Red Army.

In December 1922, the Ukrainian and Belorussian soviet republics and Transcaucasus Federation joined the Russian soviet republic in a Union of Soviet Socialist Republics. Its capital was Moscow (the old imperial capital, Petrograd, would have to get used to being second city). Its emblem was the hammer and sickle, with the motto (written in Russian,

Ukrainian, Belorussian, Georgian, Armenian, and Azeri): 'Proletarians of the world, unite!'

The Constitution of the new Union gave the republics the right to secede, although for close to seventy years, none ever invoked that right. In the 1920s and '30s, five additional Central Asian republics (Uzbekistan, Turkmenistan, Tajikistan, Kazakhstan and Kirgizstan) were carved out of the RSFSR, and the Transcaucasus Federation split into its three constituent parts: Georgia, Armenia and Azerbaijan. In 1939, the three Baltic states (Latvia, Lithuania and Estonia) and Moldavia were incorporated into the Soviet Union as a result of secret clauses of the 1939 Nazi–Soviet Pact, bringing the total number of republics in the Union to fifteen.

The Soviet Union was clearly a successor state to Imperial Russia, albeit with a slightly diminished territory. Whether that meant that it, too, was an empire – with Russians ruling a bunch of internal colonies in the form of national republics – was a matter of dispute. The Western powers, hostile to the Bolshevik regime and hoping for its downfall, saw it as an empire, and an illegitimate one at that. The Bolsheviks, however, had a completely different way of seeing their Union. Many of the party's leadership were not Russian at all but belonged to one of the old Russian Empire's oppressed minorities, such as Latvians, Poles, Georgians, Armenians and Jews. They were sworn enemies of Russian imperialism who had grown up resenting increasing discrimination against non-Russians in the last years of the Empire. They saw their role inside and outside the Soviet Union as one of liberating former colonial subjects, particularly in Asia (including the

Central Asian territories conquered by the Russian Empire in the nineteenth century). According to the mantra of the 1920s, 'Russian chauvinism' was the 'greatest danger', meaning that of all nationalisms in the Soviet Union, the one that was pernicious was the Russian.

The Bolsheviks were committed Marxist internationalists for whom nationalism was false consciousness. Nonetheless, they recognised its popular appeal and its tendency to multiply in response to attempts to eradicate it. The Bolsheviks were not going to make that mistake: their strategy was to *encourage* non-Russian nationalisms, not only through administrative use of the native language and furthering of national cultures but also through the creation of separate territorial administrations, starting at the level of republic (for example, Ukraine) and going right down to the level of village Soviet (there was an array of Jewish, Belorussian, Russian, Latvian, Greek and other 'autonomous districts' within the Ukrainian republic). It was one of the paradoxes of Soviet rule that its administrative structures not only protected national identities but also helped to create them.

THE PROBLEM OF BACKWARDNESS

The Bolsheviks were modernisers and rationalisers through and through: modernisation in the form of state-led industrial development was their core program and a large part of what they meant by socialism. They considered Russia's backwardness vis-a-vis the West as a great challenge to be overcome, yet in their analysis, Russia also had its own internal 'Orient' – Central Asia – to modernise and civilise via capital investment in infrastructure and industry as well as literacy schools and affirmative action programs. For the Union as a whole, modernisation and the jettisoning of tradition were high on the short-term as well as the long-term agenda. Imperial Russia's Julian calendar, thirteen days behind the Gregorian calendar used in the West, was an early victim (meaning that once the calendar changed in 1918, the 'October Revolution' was commemorated on 7 November). Changes to the old orthography, emancipation of women from a range of legal shackles, legalisation of abortion, no-fault divorce, disestablishment of the Orthodox Church (seen as a particularly egregious repository of superstition) and abolition of social estates were all introduced within months of the Bolsheviks' seizing power.

How backward was Russia before the Revolution? 'Backwardness' is a slippery concept that always implies a comparison with something admired as more advanced; in Russia's case, the comparison was with Western Europe. Pulling Russia out of backwardness and into the West had been Peter the Great's mantra two centuries earlier, and building the new capital, St Petersburg (as close as possible to Europe), and forcibly shaving the boyars' beards were among his strategies. Russia had done well enough under Peter's successors – notably Catherine the Great, correspondent of the Enlightenment philosophers Diderot and Voltaire – to be recognised as a Great Power in Europe by the early nineteenth century, a reputation solidified by the defeat of Napoleon's armies on Russia's steppes. Its territories increased in the course of the nineteenth century as it expanded southwards into the Caucasus and overran small Central Asia sovereign states ruled by khans to the east. But it was not until

Moscow's Red Square as it looked around 1900. Note that the name predates the Communists ('red' connoting beautiful). St Basil's is on the left, the Kremlin on the right.

Moscow's Lubyanka Square as it looked around 1900. It was renamed Dzerzhinsky Square in 1926.

the early 1860s that the peasants were emancipated from serf-dom as part of Alexander II's Great Reforms. The country was also a latecomer to the industrial revolution: Russia's industrial take-off was in the 1890s, half a century behind Britain, and it relied heavily on state sponsorship (like Japan in the same period) and foreign investment.

At the time of Russia's first modern census in 1897, the Empire's population was 126 million, of which ninety-two million lived in European Russia (including what is now Ukraine and the eastern part of Poland). The rest was divided between the Empire's Polish provinces and the Caucasus, both with around nine million, followed by Siberia and Central Asia. While the urban population of European Russia had tripled between 1863 and 1914, the degree of urbanisation and indus-trialisation sharply declined the further one moved away from the Western frontier, the Polish provinces being by far the most developed region of the Empire. In Siberia, 92 per cent of the population was rural. Less than a third of the Empire's population in the ten-to-fifty-nine age group was literate, but this masked substantial disparities between men and women, urban and rural, young and old. Among people in their twen-ties, 45 per cent of men were literate, though only 12 per cent of women; for people in their fifties, the male literacy rate was 26 per cent with the female a mere 1 per cent.

In addition to the highly developed cities of Warsaw and Riga (which would be lost to the Soviet Union after the Revolu-tion), the Union had a rapidly growing mining and metallur-gical industry in the Donbass region of what is now Ukraine, much of it foreign-owned, with a workforce recruited largely

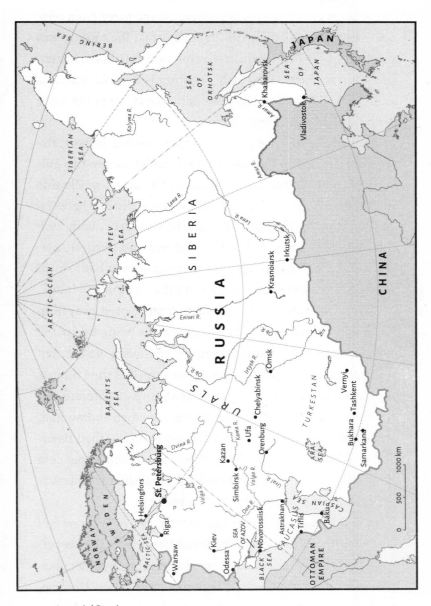

Imperial Russia

from villages in Russia. St Petersburg, Moscow, Kiev, Kharkov and the port city of Odessa on the Black Sea were also industrialising, while Baku (in Azerbaijan, on the Caspian Sea) was becoming a major oil centre.

For administrative and census purposes, the population was still divided into social estates (*sosloviia*) – nobility, clergy and townspeople, and peasantry, each group with its own rights and duties to the Tsar – although such estates had long vanished in Western Europe and struck Russia's Western-oriented intelligentsia as an embarrassing anachronism. The peasantry, at 77 per cent, was by far the largest estate, with townspeople and other urban estates accounting for only 11 per cent. The intelligentsia, or educated class, was a modern anomaly not accommodated by the estate scheme.

While Russia was a multinational empire, the concept of nationality was too modern for the tsarist regime, and the 1897 census gathered information only on religious confession and native language. 'Russian' was the language claimed by two-thirds of the Empire's population, but that included what we would now call Ukrainian and Belorussian speakers: only 44 per cent were listed as 'Great Russians'. As for religion, about 70 per cent were Russian Orthodox (including a couple of million Old Believers who had split off from the church in the seventeenth century), with 11 per cent Muslim, 9 per cent Roman Catholic and 4 per cent Jewish.

In Western Europe, particularly Britain, Russia became a byword for unenlightened autocracy, a process helped by energetic propaganda from exiled Russian revolutionaries benefiting from Britain's generous asylum policies. The tsarist practice of exiling dissidents to Siberia was known and reviled throughout the 'civilised' world, just as Gulag would be during the Cold War. Despite its size and great power status, the precariousness of tsarist power became evident when in 1905, following humiliating defeat in a war with Japan, it barely survived a revolution that covered the breadth of its territory and took more than a year to quell. The revolution of 1905 provided Russian radicals with a heroic legend and a spontaneously generated revolutionary institution, the popularly elected soviet (literally, council), combining executive and legislative powers. Lev Trotsky, a Marxist of the Menshevik faction, achieved instant fame as the charismatic leader of the Petersburg Soviet, but the Bolshevik leader Vladimir Lenin, returning like Trotsky from emigration, arrived late for the revolution in 1905 and played only an inconspicuous part.

REVOLUTIONARIES IN WAITING

If you wanted to have a revolution in Russia, looking to the downtrodden peasantry for support might have seemed the obvious course. That was indeed the reasoning of the first generation of revolutionaries, the so-called Narodniks (Populists) who dominated the radical scene in the 1860s and '70s. Mindful of the long tradition of peasant revolt in Russia, they saw the peasants as potential overthrowers of the Tsars as well as a source of untainted moral wisdom. But peasants gave Narodnik emissaries short shrift, perceiving them as members of an urban elite with which they had nothing in common. It was disappointment at that rejection that paved the way for the rise of Marxism in the revolutionary movement in the 1880s. Disciples of the German socialist thinkers Karl Marx and Friedrich

Engels, the Russian Marxists offered a 'scientific prediction' of the inexorable 'necessity' of revolution, since capitalism was historically predestined to give way to socialism. The industrial proletariat, generated by the processes of capitalism itself, was the revolutionary agent chosen by history, meaning that the peasantry became (at least theoretically) irrelevant. Commitment to the revolution, previously justified on moral grounds, was reconfigured as something closer to a rational choice, rooted in an understanding of historical necessity (*Gesetzmässigkeit* in German and *zakonomernost'* in Russian – but in the English-speaking world, an alien concept). These were deep philosophical waters, truly grasped only by the chosen few, but all Russian, and later Soviet, Marxists knew what *zakonomerno* meant: that was when things went as, in principle, they were supposed to (as distinct from the 'accidental' and 'spontaneous' way they often went in practice).

Marxist revolutionaries in Russia identified with the industrial working class, but initially most of them were offspring of the nobility or the intelligentsia. As in other developing countries in the late nineteenth and twentieth centuries, higher education in Russia meant Westernisation, which often brought radicalisation as a by-product; the first characteristic (Westernisation) implied alienation from the local population, the second (radicalisation) a sense of mission to lead it. Educated Russians with radical ideas had largely appropriated the term 'intelligentsia' for themselves, contemptuously excluding people with the same kind of education who went on to work for the state. (The fact that Alexander II's Great Reforms had been carefully drafted by a group of 'enlightened bureaucrats' working behind the scenes did not affect this judgement: what were mere reforms when thoroughgoing revolution and spiritual rebirth were needed?) It was the intelligentsia's self-appointed function to criticise the government (*any* government, as became clear after the collapse of tsarism) and act as the conscience of the society, and this, of course, brought it into constant conflict with the imperial authorities, notably the Okhrana, or secret police. For most, radical politics was not a day job. But a minority became full-time professional revolutionaries, often during their student days, which soon led to arrests, prison terms, exile within Russia, escape from exile (not that difficult) and, if parental funds permitted it, emigration. All the revolutionary factions, no matter whether they declared their social base to be peasants or workers, were led by revolutionary intellectuals, most of whom had spent long years in emigration in Europe.

Vladimir Lenin, born Vladimir Ulyanov in 1870 in the Volga town of Simbirsk (renamed Ulyanovsk in 1924 after Lenin's death and still, rather surprisingly, bearing that name), was a law student in Kazan when he became radicalised, partly by the execution of his elder brother for involvement in a plot against the emperor. The Ulyanovs were professional middle class in our terms (the father an inspector of schools who rose high enough to become non-hereditary nobility) and mainly Russian in terms of ethnicity, though there was some German and Jewish in the mix. Lenin's embrace of revolution brought him into the Marxist League of Struggle for the Emancipation of the Working Class in St Petersburg, which won him the usual punishment of administrative exile within Russia, followed by voluntary exile outside Russia, supported financially by his mother. He joined the motley group of Russian and other Eastern European revolutionaries who congregated in London, Paris, Geneva, Zurich and Berlin – a world full of seedy lodging houses, passionate hairsplitting arguments with other revolutionaries, police spies, informers, loneliness and long hours spent in libraries.

Within his Marxist revolutionary group, ethnic Russians like Lenin and his wife, Nadezhda Krupskaya, were less numerous than Jews, Poles, Latvians and other members of national minorities within the Russian Empire, who, from the late nineteenth century, were increasingly harassed by

Vladimir, a schoolboy, is front right in this 1879 studio portrait of the Ulyanov family; his older brother Alexander (to be executed as a terrorist at the age of twenty-one) stands at left.

Imperial Russian authorities and subject to policies of Russification. Lenin was notable in revolutionary circles for his intransigence and need to dominate his own small faction, which became known as the Bolsheviks after a split in the social democratic movement engineered by Lenin in 1903. The term 'Bolshevik' was derived from the Russian for 'majority', while their opponents were labelled 'Mensheviks', from the Russian for 'minority' – a neat sleight of hand on Lenin's part, as it was actually the Mensheviks who were in the majority.

Russian Marxists had a basic problem: according to the Marxist understanding of the laws of history, 'their' revolution – the one to which they had dedicated their lives – was not next on the historical agenda, but the one after next. This was because Russia was still only at the beginning of the capitalist phase, with a bourgeoisie too weak or passive to have carried out the bourgeois liberal revolution against the autocracy that was historically overdue. As a result, unlike Britain and Germany, it was not yet 'ripe' for proletarian socialist revolution. The Mensheviks, apart from some mavericks like Trotsky, took this immaturity argument seriously (probably their major doctrinal difference with Lenin); the Bolsheviks in practice did not. But it would be wrong to accept at face value the Mensheviks' claims that the Bolsheviks were consequently bad Marxists. As their actions in power would later demonstrate, a Marxist understanding of class war and historical necessity was deeply ingrained in the party leaders, and, moreover, there were Marxist ways of justifying the legitimacy of proletarian revolution in Russia (the theory that the weakest link in the imperialist chain would be the first to snap, for example). The truth was that any revolutionary worth his salt was going to find a way round the theoretical prohibition on revolution.

Another problem for Marxist revolutionaries was the comparative weakness of the Russian proletariat. True, the proletariat was highly concentrated in large-scale enterprises (a revolutionary plus), but its number was still embarrassingly small, a bit over three million in 1914, out of a total population already over 125 million in 1897. This weakness was partly compensated by Lenin's concept of the revolutionary party, which was to consist of full-time revolutionaries and act as the 'vanguard' of the proletariat. It was the task of the vanguard to open workers' eyes to their historic revolutionary mission, and these workers – now labelled 'conscious' – would in turn act as a vanguard for the unenlightened but often rebellious masses. According to Russian police observations in 1901, the Bolsheviks were having some success with this project: the police noted that in the working-class milieu, 'the easygoing Russian young man has been transformed into a special type of semiliterate "intelligent", who feels obliged to spurn family and religion, to disregard the law and to deny and scoff at constituted authority', and such people acquire authority over the 'inert mass of workers'.

Lenin was the most uncompromisingly revolutionary within the Russian Marxist emigration, as well as the most authoritarian – intolerant of challenges within his faction, and insistent on the importance of organisation and professional leadership in the revolutionary movement, as opposed to popular spontaneity. But he was not a one-dimensional character. Married to Krupskaya, who was a teacher and educational theorist by vocation, he shared, at least to some degree, her conviction that enlightenment of the people was the deep purpose of revolution, making the provision of schools, literacy classes and libraries for the masses a key revolutionary task. To be sure, Lenin, unlike Krupskaya, was a natural politician with a strong sense of mission, for whom faction fighting and the struggle for power were the stuff of life. It was mainly during political doldrums that he had time to worry about popular enlightenment.

WORLD WAR I AND REVOLUTION

In January 1917, in exile in Zurich, Lenin lamented that he did not expect to see the Russian Revolution in his lifetime. It was a reasonable judgement that turned out to be wrong. The war years had not been a source of much pleasure to him, or to the international socialist movement in general. The hope had been that if war broke out between the imperialist competitors, workers would refuse to back the government and fire on their fellow proletarians. What happened was the opposite: workers and many socialist intellectuals suddenly became patriots, falling into line with their governments and being swept up in the intense nationalist enthusiasm that marked the early stages of the war. Lenin was unusual in continuing to hold that this was an imperialist war in which workers had no stake, and moreover arguing that for the Russian revolutionary cause, the best outcome would be Russia's defeat. It was not a popular view among his émigré colleagues, and the Bolshevik Party fragmented further.

Russia's military unpreparedness quickly became evident – the Imperial Army didn't even have enough rifles for its initial call-up – and by 1915, with the Germans transferring forces to the Eastern Front, enemy troops had taken much of the Empire's western provinces. The defeats, occupations and evacuations were shocking to the initially patriotic public. Two and a half million Russian POWs were in German hands by the end of the war, and there were almost two million military casualties, not counting the vast numbers wounded and invalided, and an only slightly smaller number of civilian casualties. As of February 1917, the army had conscripted a total of over fifteen million men, mainly peasants, leaving women to till the fields on their own. In the face of the German threat to the Empire's western provinces, the Russian army deported perhaps as many as one million Jews to the interior of the country (the Pale of Settlement, in which most Jews were required to live, was close to the western border) as well as a quarter of a million Russo-Germans; in addition, six million refugees fled eastwards into the Russian hinterland to avoid the fighting.

Discontent was rising among the political and military elites as well as the hard-pressed civilian population and the battered ranks of the conscript army. It was rumoured that Emperor Nicholas II, an inept and indecisive figure, was under the thrall of his wife, Empress Alexandra, and their shady protégé Grigory Rasputin, who claimed to have healing powers over their haemophiliac child, Alexei, heir to the throne. Rasputin was murdered in December 1916 by the dissolute young Prince Felix Yusupov, who saw himself as defending the autocracy. Senior officers in the army were sufficiently alarmed by the situation to start talking to leaders of the recently created Duma (a parliament that was a product of the 1905 revolution). They collectively decided that Nicholas, who clearly did not enjoy the role of ruler, should be asked to abdicate on his own behalf and that of Alexei in favour of a brother who, it was hoped, would provide stronger leadership. Nicholas agreed and abdicated, but the brother turned the plotters down, leaving them confused and without a Plan B. That was the February Revolution, occurring in early March according to our calendar, which the Marxists labelled 'bourgeois liberal' (despite the fact that the plotters mainly belonged to the nobility and few were liberals). The February Revolution produced a stop-gap institution unpromisingly called the Provisional Government, which undertook to call a Constituent Assembly at some future time to decide how Russia should be governed. The Allies, desperate to keep Russia fighting in the war, immediately recognised the new government. That was one of the few things going for it.

The mood of rank-and-file conscripts in the army was grim. This was largely because of casualties, defeats and the unexpectedly long time away from home, but resentment at the Tsar's removal in 1914 of the traditional vodka allowance for soldiers no doubt played a part. The prohibition, applied to the civilian population as well, removed an important source of state revenue and caused a diversion of grain to the illegal making of home-brew, which in turn produced bread shortages. A wave of popular discontent in the winter of 1916–1917 started with women workers queuing for bread in Petrograd (the capital had been renamed at the start of the war because 'St Petersburg' sounded too German) and spread into the armed forces, from which men sick of being cannon fodder started to desert. As the spring agricultural sowing drew nearer, more and more peasant soldiers left for their villages, their officers proving powerless to stop them. In the big cities, police started to melt away when faced with the growing crowds celebrating the Tsar's abdication. It was a classic revolutionary situation – not because the forces of revolution were irresistible, even in the big cities where protest was strongest, but because the old regime had lost that mysterious thing called legitimacy, both with the populace and the elite, and its army and police had stopped being reliable protectors.

The heady moment of liberation associated with the February Days remained long in popular memory. Now there was

Revolutionary demonstration in Petrograd, February 1917. The banner reads: ' Freedom, equality, brotherhood.'

revolution on the streets, or at least cheering demonstrators, and *mirabile dictu* for the Marxists, many of them were workers. An improvised popular body, modelled on the Petersburg Soviet of 1905 and consisting of deputies directly elected in factories and army units, came into being more or less at the same time as the Provisional Government. When the Petrograd Soviet declared itself the representative of popular revolution, demanding the right to co-sign any instructions to the army, the latter saw no choice but to comply. Thus the 'dual power' came into being – in essence a power-sharing arrangement between the Provisional Government and the Petrograd Soviet. It was a remarkable institutional expression of the belief of the Soviet's socialist leaders (initially mainly Mensheviks) that as Russia was not yet ripe for proletarian revolution, the bourgeois liberals should have their historically mandated term – under the watchful eye of the proletariat.

Within the revolutionary movement, the general mood was exalted, self-congratulatory and supportive of socialist unity. But there was a lone dissenter: Lenin. It took him a month or more to return from Zurich across the front (the war, of course, was still in progress), but he and a number of other revolutionaries finally got the Germans to permit transit of the famous 'sealed train' across German territory to Sweden and thence via Finland to Russia. He arrived at Petrograd's Finland Station in April, greeted by an enthusiastic crowd, including reconciliation-minded socialists from the Soviet. Lenin quickly put an end to the happy mood of unity. There should be no more power-sharing with the Provisional Government, he announced. His new slogan, 'All power to the soviets!', meant forgetting about the bourgeois liberal revolution that the other Marxists thought Russia had to have and going straight to proletarian revolution. It was not just the Mensheviks who were appalled. So were those of Lenin's own Bolshevik faction who had reached the capital earlier and basically fallen into line with the socialist united front. Even Lenin's wife was startled: 'Ilyich has gone crazy,' she was reported to have muttered, sotto voce, to an old comrade standing nearby.

The next months saw the economic situation worsen, desertions from the army increase and huge demonstrations of workers and soldiers and sailors from garrisons near the capitals filling Petrograd and Moscow streets; the Provisional Government and the army high command made a desperate attempt to get the army in shape for summer fighting. In Petrograd, where the political action was, the Bolsheviks' intransigent stance appealed to the demonstrators, their membership and influence shot up, and some action-oriented Mensheviks like Trotsky broke ranks to join the Bolsheviks. But in the crackdown after the biggest demonstration in early July, Lenin felt obliged to flee to Finland to avoid arrest. Alexander Kerensky, a lawyer from a minor socialist party, took over the leadership of the Provisional Government from Prince Lvov, but the situation in the army and the capital failed to improve and the Germans continued to advance, taking Riga (Latvia's capital, still part of the Russian Empire) in August. This brought German forces uncomfortably close to Petrograd.

In September came high drama: an attempted military coup led by General Lavr Kornilov, recently appointed commander-in-chief by Kerensky and charged with the task of restoring discipline in the military. The relationship of Kornilov and Kerensky was murky, as that of Mikhail Gorbachev and the coup leaders of August 1990 would be seventy-three years later: it is possible that Kornilov saw himself acting for Kerensky rather than against him. In any case, the coup failed, owing to the prompt action of railway workers who stopped his echelons reaching the capital, and Kerensky's standing was fatally damaged.

Lenin, supported by Trotsky, decided that the time had come to make the bid for power that demonstrators on the streets had been calling for since July. The October Revolution was achieved almost as quietly in Petrograd as the February Revolution had been, although later legends made it a much more daring and bloody affair. With a national Congress of Soviets assembled at a girls' school in Petrograd, and Trotsky having done the necessary preparatory work within the Petrograd Soviet, Lenin emerged from his Finnish hide-out and announced that the Bolsheviks were leading a soviet takeover of power and abolishing the Provisional Government. The Mensheviks walked out of the congress, but it was a gesture that damaged only themselves. Kerensky, having donned women's clothes as disguise, was already in flight.

A surprise awaited those who thought that 'all power to the soviets' meant that some soviet body – the Petrograd Soviet, perhaps, or some executive agency elected by the Congress of Soviets – would take over the leadership of the country. It turned out – and many Bolsheviks were among those surprised – that the new government was to be a Council of People's Commissars (in effect, a state cabinet) whose just-appointed members were read out to the congress by Lenin's spokesman: all were Bolsheviks, with Lenin as chairman. The Bolsheviks had taken power.

ESTABLISHMENT OF BOLSHEVIK RULE AND CIVIL WAR

While the Bolsheviks would have passionately rejected the thought, October had been an easy victory. Failure in war had discredited the old regime, and failure to get out of the war had done the same for the Provisional Government. Wartime exigencies concentrated millions of discontented men (with arms) in cities and garrisons, giving the revolutionaries a large constituency to draw on. The industrial working class, too, was highly concentrated in a relatively small number of big cities – making the task of revolutionary organisation there easier. And on top of that, many of Russia's largest capitalist enterprises had been foreign-owned, meaning that some of their owners and managers had already left at the outbreak of war and the remainder were much easier to dislodge than if they had been locals. But of course, the seizure of power in Petrograd in October was only the beginning. It remained to be seen whether the Bolsheviks could hold onto this power, extend it to the rest of Russia and learn how to govern.

With Marxist punctiliousness, the Bolsheviks described their newly established rule as a 'dictatorship of the proletariat' whose task, with the 'vanguard' party as its instrument, was to carry the country forward through the transitional period until it was ready for socialism. Socialist critics might quibble about whether it was really the proletariat that was now in power, but in the circumstances of the civil war (which broke out in mid-1918 and continued for more than two years), the question of the party's proletarian credentials was a secondary one. Dictatorship was the more salient concept, and in effect – despite some quasi-parliamentary trimmings – it was a dictatorship of the Bolshevik Party. The Bolsheviks expected opposition from the old governing and land-owning classes and the urban bourgeoisie, and they were open about the fact that terror would be used against such 'class enemies'; the Cheka – the acronym for the All-Russian Extraordinary Commission for Struggle against Counter-Revolution, Sabotage and Speculation – was set up in December 1917 to deal with them.

In the name of social justice, the Cheka practiced forcible 'expropriation' of the property of the bourgeoisie and nobility, including their houses and apartments. There was no shortage of lower-class volunteers for expropriation brigades; indeed, one of the Bolsheviks' minor problems in 1917–1918 was that common criminals had got in on the act, showing up at the door of bourgeois apartments as expropriators on their own behalf rather than the state's and turning confiscation into a private enterprise. When this came to the Bolsheviks' attention, they denounced the offenders as 'lumpen proletarians' rather than true members of the working class. But as lumpen was simply a Marxist pejorative for proletarians who lacked the proper socialist consciousness, it was difficult for an outsider to tell the lumpen proletarians from the real ones.

Much of this revolutionary action was taking place in the big cities where Bolshevik control was firmest. In the countryside, independent of any effective state control, the peasants were settling scores in their own way, driving out landlords and burning down their manor houses. When that had been largely accomplished, they often turned on the more prosperous members of their own communities, the so-called *kulaks*, and, in the newly fashionable terminology, 'expropriated' them.

The civil war was bloody and brutal on both sides, leaving complex legacies of bitterness and grievance. Jews in the western regions of the country were subjected to pogroms whose savagery exceeded those of the late tsarist period. Anarchy and confusion reigned in the provinces. 'White' (anti-Bolshevik) armies, led by officers of the old Imperial Army and more or less actively supported by Russia's former wartime allies (Britain, France and the United States) and Japan, formed on the peripheries, hoping to overthrow the Bolsheviks and restore the old regime. In the Ukrainian provinces, Ukrainian nationalists, Bolsheviks, anarchists and Whites established precarious regimes (the capital, Kiev, changed hands five times in a year) in the context of German and later Polish military incursions. Mensheviks took power in Georgia in mid-1918, fighting Ottoman Turks and Armenians; Bolsheviks set up a commune in Baku whose leaders were executed by the British. A short-lived Volga Republic came into being in Samara, courtesy of trainloads of armed Czech prisoners of war (socialists but anti-Bolshevik), who were on their way to Vladivostok on the Pacific with the intention of sailing round the world to join the Allied military effort on the Western Front. The Japanese sent tens of thousands of troops into the Russian maritime provinces and Siberia.

The Bolsheviks had managed at great cost to pull Russia out of the European war in the spring of 1918, and the punitive treaty they signed with the Germans at Brest-Litovsk would have deprived them of much valuable territory in Ukraine, had it not become null and void on the Germans' defeat by the remaining Allies eight months later. But the Bolsheviks had not yet escaped the meshes of war, since civil war broke out within half a year of their seizure of power. Nor, arguably, did they altogether wish to escape. Up to this point, military valour had had no part in the Bolshevik pantheon of virtues; there was not even a paramilitary tradition. Yet a zest for fighting the 'White' enemy quickly emerged in the party and among its supporters, and Lenin himself, though he never acquired the military patina embraced by many of his colleagues, probably thought that victory in civil war was a good way of legitimising Bolshevik rule. In any case, there would have been no avoiding civil war, even without the provocation of the execution of the Tsar and his family in the Urals capital of Ekaterinburg in mid-1918 (by local Bolsheviks, but with at least tacit approval from the centre). Officers of the dispersed Imperial Army, now jobless, wanted a fight, and the Allies, freed from November 1918 from the demands of the European war, were happy to provide backup.

For their part, the Bolsheviks managed the significant feat, under Trotsky's leadership, of creating a new 'Red Army' that by the end of the civil war was five million strong, the country's major employer and, in many parts of the country, the effective administrative power rather than the nominal civilian institutions. This was made possible by the fact that, given the way the civil war was fought, with small episodic engagements rather than large-scale bloody confrontations across trenches, the chances of dying were much less than for conscripts in the old

Trotsky, represented as a Red devil in a White Army propaganda poster
entitled 'Peace and Freedom in the Soviet Land'

imperial forces, and the Bolsheviks were relatively tolerant of
deserters (who often showed up again after the sowing or har-
vest). In any case, only a minority of those on army rations were
actually combat troops. The Whites, with officers aplenty, had
more difficulty than the Reds recruiting rank-and-file soldiers;
and the support they had from the Allies, while not enough to
turn the military tide, was sufficiently visible to arouse Russian
popular indignation against 'foreign intervention'.

The victorious outcome, achieved by the winter of 1920–1921,
is often attributed to the peasants' preference, when the chips
were down, for Reds over Whites, who they feared would
bring back the landlords. The same was probably true of the
Empire's non-Russians, unenthusiastic about the Whites'
attachment to 'Russia one and indivisible'. The White Armies,

uncoordinated and often poorly led, had the disadvantage of being scattered around the peripheries of a large country whose transport and distribution networks flowed outwards from the centre. The end of the Civil War led to an exodus of the Whites over the southern borders, with many settling in Yugoslavia, Czechoslovakia and Bulgaria, and over the eastern borders to China, where many ended up in Harbin, in effect a Russian city in Manchuria. The emigration of between one and two million people, including many from the elites, constituted a very substantial loss of talent for the new regime, but also the permanent removal of a political threat.

As of the beginning of 1921, there was a bit of mopping up to do in Central Asia, the Caucasus and the Far East, but the outcome of the civil war was clear: the Reds had won, and the territory they ruled was not hugely reduced from that of the old Russian Empire. The Baltic states and Finland had been allowed to depart. The Polish provinces – the most urbanised and industrialised part of the old Empire – had been lost after a military clash between the Red Army and the forces of the new Polish state that resulted in the Red Army's defeat and a useful lesson for the Bolshevik leaders: when Polish workers saw Soviet troops advancing on Warsaw in 1921, they perceived them as Russian invaders rather than proletarian liberators.

As of 1922, the Communist Party membership comprised 72 per cent Great Russians, 6 per cent Ukrainians, 5 per cent Jews, 3 per cent Latvians and 2 per cent Georgians. That meant that about three of every thousand Soviet citizens of all nationalities were Communist Party members, with Jews, Georgians and Russians somewhat over-represented according to population share and Ukrainians under-represented. The strong preponderance of Russians in the party was a product of civil war recruitment, which brought total numbers up from 24,000 in 1917 to over 700,000 in March 1921, and made it a mass party for the first time. It was also, in contrast to the situation before 1917, overwhelmingly a *men's* party, with memories of fighting in the civil war as the bonding agent. At the beginning of 1922, women made up under 8 per cent of party membership.

The Bolshevik leaders felt a degree of unease about the Union's territorial similarity with the old Empire and the possibility of being misrecognised as Russian imperialists by its erstwhile subjects. Lenin repeatedly urged kid-glove treatment of non-Russians and avoidance of 'even the slightest rudeness or injustice' that might be misconstrued in national terms. He clashed with Stalin about how to handle the Georgians, the most obstreperous territorially based nationality left now that the Poles were gone. Stalin, a Georgian himself, was less tolerant of those Georgian Communists whose prickly national pride was offended by being subsumed in the Transcaucasus Federation. From his point of view, it was all pretty simple: if the peripheries of the old Russian Empire were lost to the new revolutionary state, that would only damage the international revolutionary movement, since they 'would inevitably fall into the cabal of international imperialism'. So it was a binary choice: '*either* with Russia, which means liberation from the imperialist yoke, *or* with the Entente, which means the imperialist yoke is inevitable imperialist. There is no third option'. Their union on the territory of the old Russian Empire would be the first step on the way to a 'World Socialist Soviet Republic'.

MURDER OF THE ROMANOV FAMILY, 1918

Ipatiev House in 1928

In the spring of 1918, the Bolsheviks stashed away the Tsar (now referred to as Nikolai Romanov) and his family in a two-storey dwelling, known as Ipatiev House after its former 'bourgeois' owner, in the Urals city of Ekaterinburg. The original intention was to put the former ruler on public trial in Moscow, but civil war intervened. On 17 September 1918 – a week before Ekaterinburg fell to anti-Bolshevik forces – Nikolai and his whole family (wife Alexandra, daughters Olga, Tatyana, Maria and Anastasia, and the young haemophiliac heir, Alexei) were shot in the cellar and their bodies disposed of in the forest. This was not a rogue local decision, but a considered action, coordinated with Moscow, and motivated by fear that the Tsar and his heir would fall into White monarchist hands. The Bolshevik leaders announced the execution of the Tsar, but not of the rest of the family, giving rise to endless rumours that at least one of the royal daughters (usually Anastasia) had survived. The death of the Romanovs was ancient history by 1977, when Boris Yeltsin, then Urals party leader, ordered the demolition of Ipatiev House. But that ancient history became modern again during perestroika; and it was under Yeltsin's post-Soviet presidency that the Russian Orthodox Church planned the construction of a grand 'Church on Blood in the Name of All Saints' on the site of Ipatiev House. This shrine to the now-canonised Romanovs looks across the river to the equally grand Boris Yeltsin Presidential Centre, opened in 2015 and dedicated to democracy.

SOVIET RE-INVENTION

One way of fitting yourself into the new world was to change your name, which in the early days of revolutionary permissiveness was easy. *Barrikada* (barricade) and *Iskra* (the name of Lenin's pre-revolutionary newspaper) were popular, along with *Kim* (not after Kipling, but the Russian acronym for the Communist International). Civil War political commissar Medvedev named his twins *Roy* (for the Indian revolutionary, M. N. Roy) and *Zhores* (for the French socialist Jean Jaurès). *Vladlen* and *Ninel* (both from Lenin) were in vogue, along with *Edison* and *Electron* (in homage to modern technology). People also gave up 'peasant' names like Tit and Fekla in favour of the aristocratic *Konstantin* and *Natalia*, probably taking their cue from Lev Tolstoy's novels and other Russian classics that were a staple of the Soviet school curriculum.

Class origins needed adjustment, too. After being rejected for Komsomol membership on class grounds, Raisa Orlova, a young Muscovite from the intelligentsia, concluded that

> there was something inferior and insufficiently firm within me. I was an 'intellectual', and had to struggle against it without fail. I had to weed it out.

Children of priests placed advertisements in newspapers stating that they were 'renouncing' their fathers; one desperate Communist, saddled with a father who was both a noble and former Tsarist policeman, murdered him. A Tatar peasant woman married to a kulak took the less drastic course of divorce, framed in terms of women's emancipation: she claimed that for the twenty years of her marriage, given her husband's exploitative nature, she had not shared his kulak status but been 'nothing but a female hired hand (*batrachka*)'.

2

THE LENIN YEARS AND THE SUCCESSION STRUGGLE

THE WAY THE BOLSHEVIKS WROTE THE HISTORY, they surged into power as the party of the industrial working class. That wasn't pure fantasy – the crowds on the streets of Moscow and Petrograd in July were for them, and the party had had an influx of new members. In October 1917, they had the largest number of delegates in the elected national Congress of Soviets. In the elections to the Constituent Assembly held in November, they ran second, with 25 per cent of the national vote, to the peasant-oriented Socialist Revolutionary (SR) party – but by December that party had split, with several left SRs entering Lenin's government.

The Bolsheviks' notion of representation, however, was a distinctly non-parliamentary one. They saw their party as the chosen representative of the working class, and in their mind, this was a one-off historic choice, an indissoluble union. The Bolsheviks could not conceive of the possibility that workers might turn to other political representatives if they became dissatisfied with the new regime. But under the prevailing dire economic and military circumstances, such dissatisfaction was extremely likely. In fact, it was manifest, along with renewed worker interest in other (socialist) political parties as early as the spring of 1918. By the end of 1920, the Kronstadt sailors – early and firm supporters of the Bolsheviks in 1917 – had come out in revolt, calling for 'soviets without Communists' (the Bolsheviks had renamed themselves as the Russian Communist party in 1918 and would become the Communist Party of the Soviet Union in 1924). The Kronstadt revolt was a terrible symbolic repudiation for the Bolsheviks, but it did not turn them from their path. The power to lead Russia out of backwardness into socialism via 'proletarian dictatorship' had fallen into their hands, and they were not about to let it drop.

Worker dissatisfaction was not the Bolsheviks' only problem with the working class. There was the more alarming possibility that the class itself was unravelling. Soldiers and sailors of the Imperial Army, serving as temporary proletarians throughout the revolutionary year, had demobilised. As for industrial workers, some were now on the wrong side of the western border, and many of those who remained in Russia and Ukraine had disconcertingly vanished from the cities, going back to their native villages to survive on their family plots. This was not how proletarians were meant to behave, according to Marx, and it had been easy for the Bolsheviks to forget that Russia's first-generation proletariat still had strong ties to the peasantry, which meant that when factories shut down and hunger ravaged the towns, they had the option of simply going home and becoming peasants again. Of the 'conscious' workers actively supporting the

Bolsheviks, many had volunteered for the Red Army or had gone on to full-time party work. As the civil war ended, the victors looked around for the class that was meant to be their social support and found it gone. 'Permit me to congratulate you on being the vanguard of a non-existent class,' mocked a political opponent.

Relations with the peasantry were rocky, but this at least was a predictable problem. The Bolsheviks had retrospectively sanctioned the peasants' spontaneous land seizures, which improved their standing in rural areas, but their requisitioning of grain to feed the cities and the army – carried out by armed workers' and soldiers' brigades that brought few if any manufactured goods to offer in return – was widely resented, as was the Bolsheviks' habit of trying to split the peasantry into opposing camps. The Bolsheviks assumed that class exploitation existed in the village just as it did in the town, with kulaks the exploiters and poor peasants their victims. But peasants mainly rejected this class model, thinking of their villages as unitary communities dealing with the outside world through the traditional village organisation, the *mir*. In Ukraine, a 'Green' peasant army under Nestor Makhno fought the Bolsheviks on the one side and the Whites on the other. In the central Russian city of Tambov, a major peasant revolt was suppressed only after the dispatch of fifty thousand Red Army troops.

At the end of the civil war, the Red Army was the backbone of the Soviet administration as well as a de facto literacy school for peasant soldiers and a training site for the recruitment of future Communist administrators ('cadres').

'Kulak and Priest', poster by Viktor Deni. Note the pig's snout on the kulak.

But the Red Army could not perform these functions indefinitely. Keen students of revolutionary history, the Bolsheviks were well aware that the French Revolution had ended when Napoleon Bonaparte, a former corporal of the Revolutionary Army that had conquered much of Europe, declared himself emperor. That was not going to happen in Russia. Two million men had been demobilised from the Red Army by early 1921, and the Politburo would soon move the army's charismatic leader, Trotsky, to other work.

The end of the civil war threw the question of how the Bolsheviks proposed to govern into sharp relief. Scarcely any thought had been given to this earlier, partly because in the early years there was a real expectation of international revolution, which would have obviated the necessity of creating a separate national revolutionary government for Russia. But by the early 1920s, it was clear that the postwar wave of revolutionary activity in Europe had collapsed and Russia would have to go it alone. Future international revolution remained an article of faith, however, and the Communist International (Comintern), set up in 1919 to unite communist parties around the world under Moscow's leadership, was there to prove it. The Soviet Union and the Comintern were now looking eastwards as well as westwards: a Congress of Peoples of the East held in Baku in September 1920 proclaimed solidarity with victims of colonial exploitation and support for their liberation movements. However, since revolution had so far triumphed only in Russia, it was now imperative to work out the arrangements for what Stalin was later to call 'socialism in one country'.

The Bolsheviks assumed that in the long term the revolution would guarantee all citizens work, free education and medical care, and social-welfare protection – but none of that could be provided on a universal basis immediately, given the poverty of the state and the chaotic aftermath of war. In the short term, what was on offer was a 'dictatorship of the proletariat'. On the one hand, this meant Bolshevik Party rule in an effectively one-party state (the left SRs had quit the government in mid-1918, while other socialist parties were gradually being squeezed out of existence); on the other, it meant preferential treatment for workers in the state's distribution of scarce resources. In common parlance, then as now, 'dictatorship' usually implied rule by one man assuming dictatorial powers: Napoleon was the historic example, and Mussolini – with a party of ideologically committed volunteers to mobilise the masses behind him – the contemporary one. Mussolini's posturings as Il Duce were much ridiculed in the Soviet press, and personal dictatorship was definitely not what Lenin had in mind. In the party's Politburo, Lenin, despite his great authority as party founder, insisted on his status as no more than the first among equals.

Lenin, however, had made himself head of the government (the Council of People's Commissars) in October 1917, and may well have envisaged this as the supreme authority in the new system. In fact, it turned out otherwise. The renaming of government ministries as 'People's Commissariats' did not disguise their line of descent from the tsarist bureaucracy, and the employment of non-Communist 'experts' further damaged their standing. The party, which quickly acquired its own parallel regional and local network, staffed by full-time Communist appointees, proved a formidable competitor for primacy. From the end of the civil war, it was usually the local party secretary who was number-one man in a given locality, with the chairman of the local soviet (now part of the state apparatus) number two. In the centre, the same process took a bit longer because of Lenin's unique authority as head of the government, but by the time of his death in 1924 it was clear that the Politburo held the dominant position.

The Politburo of the first half of the 1920s consisted of about ten people elected by the party's Central Committee (which was itself elected at more or less annual party congresses by delegates from the party's local branches). Its function was to decide on major policy issues – but in addition to policy, there was the question of appointments, an urgent task as the new regime established itself. Top party appointments, as well as government and military assignments, had to be approved by the Politburo, but below that level the party also needed a body in charge of staffing the new party bureaucracy nationwide. This was handled by the Central Committee's secretariat, headed from 1922 by General Secretary Joseph Stalin, a Politburo member. Among the key appointments under his control were the secretaries of the party at the regional and district level – the local executors of 'proletarian dictatorship'.

The proliferation of new institutions, each with its own incomprehensible acronym or initials (Tseka, Ispolkom, Sovnarkom, VTsIK), bewildered contemporaries and was spoofed in many popular anecdotes, such as the one about legendary theatre director Konstantin Stanislavsky mixing up GUM, a state department store in Moscow, with the GPU, the Cheka's successor as security police. But even revolutionary institutions have a habit of slipping into familiar patterns. As the system settled down and historical precedents quietly reasserted themselves, the office of regional and republican first party secretary came to resemble that of provincial governor in tsarist times, not least in having great local power tempered only by dependence on continuing central approval (from the party secretariat and Politburo).

As for the soviets, they fell into secondary roles. At the national level, the elected body that was to be known in the 1930s as the Supreme Soviet performed a quasi-parliamentary function, with its delegates (nominated by the party) carefully chosen to give appropriate representation to workers, peasants, members of ethnic minorities and women. For most of the interwar period, its chairman, who also served as formal head of the Soviet state, was Mikhail Kalinin, a respected party elder of working-class and peasant origins. At the local level, soviet executive committees, now staffed by centrally appointed rather than locally elected personnel, were transformed into regional and district branches of the central People's Commissariats.

In the first years, the Bolshevik leaders were struggling to invent a new system on the go and make it work. The problems were enormous, in particular that of finding trustworthy cadres who could both understand instructions and use initiative. Lenin is often credited with saying that any cook could run the government. What he actually wrote, in response to 'bourgeois' criticism, was that he was neither so stupid as to think that any cook could immediately step in and run the state without training nor so prejudiced as to assume that only people born into privilege were capable of doing so. In fact, the Bolsheviks' strategy was to use 'conscious' industrial workers – not the lowest stratum of urban society but a middling socio-economic class, probably in the top 15 per cent of the Russian population – as a prime recruitment ground for administrators. The promotion of cooks, once they were trained and raised in consciousness, could come later.

The Red Army was another important source of Bolshevik cadres. The demobilisation of the early 1920s brought a flood of non-commissioned officers and literate soldiers – exposed during their army service to Bolshevik ideas – back to the towns and villages, and ready for leadership roles. An unintended consequence was a degree of cultural militarisation of what had

Trotsky, Lenin and Kamenev shown visiting the Red Army on the Polish front of the Civil War, 5 May 1920. Note Lenin's civilian dress, while the other two are in military garb.

been a civilian-minded party. It sometimes seemed as if the fifty-year-old Lenin was the only man in the party still wearing a suit: the stereotypical Bolshevik administrator of the 1920s was a young man with civil war experience in army boots and jacket, topped with a worker's cap. (The relatively few women in such roles dressed in the same way, or at least as much like a man as possible.)

THE NEW ECONOMIC POLICY
During the civil war, the Bolsheviks had nationalised everything in sight in the towns, including trade, responding both to ideology and the practical requirements of a war economy.

Given how poorly the regime's writ ran outside the big cities, the villages were essentially left to manage their own affairs, although they were subjected to periodic requisitioning raids by the Reds (and, in the territories they held, the Whites). Rationing, introduced in the towns during the European war, remained in force, and as always happens with rationing, the black market flourished. Rampant inflation drove down the value of the currency, which some hopeful enthusiasts took to be a sign of the 'withering away of money' that Marx had predicted would occur under socialism. Administrative collapse and chaos could also be interpreted as the 'withering away of the state' attendant upon socialism, of which Lenin had written as recently as mid-1917. But, in the middle of a civil war, the withering away of the state was the last thing Lenin desired. The state needed to be strong (a proletarian dictatorship), and most urgently, it needed to function.

The Communists had won the civil war, but that was about the only bright spot on the horizon. The urban economy and industrial infrastructure were smashed. The country was under boycott from the Western powers, which had not forgiven Russia's withdrawal from the European war at a crucial moment. 'Atheistic communism' was condemned from the pulpits of the West, and horror stories of cannibalism and 'socialisation of wives' abounded. A generally unspoken subtext with particular circulation in Germany and Eastern Europe was that the wild men who had taken over Russia were a bunch of Jews, as foretold in the anti-Semitic *Protocols of the Elders of Zion*. This was a little closer to the mark than was comfortable for the Bolsheviks. No longer confined to the Pale, young Jews from the western regions flocked into Moscow and Petrograd, joined the Communist Party in substantial numbers and rose quickly in the new administration. Next to Latvians, Jews were the ethnic group most over-represented in the party. (Jews made up 4.3 per cent of party members in 1927 and 1.8 per cent of the total population.) The Central Committee elected by the Tenth Party Congress in March 1921 was multi-ethnic, like the old Russian Empire itself, and included Georgians, Jews, Ukrainians, Latvians and other nationalities, but Russians predominated. In the Politburo, however, three of the five voting members (Trotsky, Grigory Zinoviev and Lev Kamenev) were Jews, with one Georgian (Stalin) and one Russian (Lenin) – though admittedly the three candidate members (Nikolai Bukharin, Mikhail Kalinin and Vyacheslav Molotov) were Russian as well.

The Bolshevik Party was firmly committed to industrial modernisation (in Marxist terms, a precondition for socialism), and they intended to accomplish it with the help of central state economic planning, a conceptual innovation for peacetime, though practised as a wartime expedient during World War I by Germany and other belligerents. But as of 1921, there were urgent economic tasks that were way beyond the capacity of Russia's embryonic planning organs to handle. A partial restoration of the market was the only immediate option, Lenin decided, though it was to be understood as a strategic temporary retreat. Under the New Economic Policy (NEP), banks and big industrial enterprises stayed in state hands, but retail trade and small industry returned to private hands or cooperatives, and peasants were once again able to sell their produce on the market. This move was a disappointment to Communist enthusiasts, and it took all of Lenin's authority to get it through.

The result was a rapid recovery of small business and trade in the towns, but also of aspects of urban life that Bolsheviks found depressingly retrograde: restaurants frequented by 'bourgeoisie' and their fur-wearing wives, cabarets and prostitution. The Bolsheviks hated the new trading bourgeoisie, known as Nepmen, and regarded them not only as 'class enemies' but also as crooks – which was not completely far-fetched, given that the NEP economy retained many features of the black market it had replaced, including a dependence on goods removed by whatever means necessary from state

'Lenin Cleanses the Land of Scum': drawing by Viktor Deni (after Mikhail Cheremnykh), 1920. Tsars, priests and capitalists are the scum.

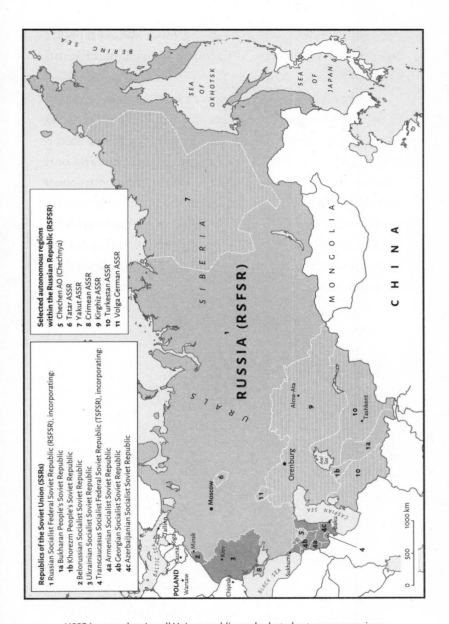

Republics of the Soviet Union (SSRs)
1 Russian Socialist Federal Soviet Republic (RSFSR), incorporating:
  1a Bukharan People's Soviet Republic
  1b Khorezm People's Soviet Republic
2 Belorussian Socialist Soviet Republic
3 Ukrainian Socialist Soviet Republic
4 Transcaucasus Socialist Federal Soviet Republic (TSFSR), incorporating:
  4a Armenian Socialist Soviet Republic
  4b Georgian Socialist Soviet Republic
  4c Azerbaijanian Socialist Soviet Republic

Selected autonomous regions within the Russian Republic (RSFSR)
5 Chechen AO (Chechnya)
6 Tatar ASSR
7 Yakut ASSR
8 Crimean ASSR
9 Kirghiz ASSR
10 Turkestan ASSR
11 Volga German ASSR

USSR in 1922, showing all Union republics and selected autonomous regions warehouses. Industry, especially large-scale industry, lagged behind, primarily because of a shortage of capital: the new Soviet state was cash-strapped, there were no local capitalists left to invest and foreign capitalists were no longer welcome.

In the non-Russian republics and regions, the main story was the integration of historically Muslim Central Asia, where the confrontation over traditional and Soviet mores focused particularly on the unveiling of women. Soviet nationality policy distinguished between 'backwards' ethnic groups (such as Uzbeks and Bashkirs) and those that were on a cultural level with (or above) the Russians (such as Ukrainians, Georgians and Jews), but 'indigenisation' – the use of local languages and the education and promotion of local cadres – was the watchword everywhere (even if in Ukraine, its implementor in the 1920s was Lazar Kaganovich, a Jew with rusty Ukrainian from a village childhood).

Some observers abroad were encouraged to hope that with NEP, Russia was recovering from its bout of revolutionary madness and returning to normal. This was exactly what the Bolshevik leaders *feared* – to have won the revolution politically, only to lose it economically and socially. Tentative feelers emerged from the West to re-establish relations on the basis of partial forgiveness of the tsarist debts (which the Bolsheviks refused to honour) and resumption of trade. But on the foreign trade question, Lenin was adamant: it should remain a state monopoly, for fear the imperialists would use it as a wedge, as in tsarist times, for pushing Russia back into a position of colonial subservience. A corollary of this attitude to foreign trade was that state borders had to be kept tightly shut to prevent the cross-border smuggling of goods that flourished in the first years after the Revolution – and later, to keep out dangerous Western ideas as well. The result of that self-imposed isolation from the world, which was to last to some degree for almost the whole life of the Soviet Union, was a kind of aggressive cultural insularity conveyed through the Soviet trademark combination of boastfulness and a sense of inferiority in dealing with the West.

Lenin insisted that relaxing economic policies did not mean political relaxation. It was just like an army engaged in tactical retreat, he wrote: discipline must be unwavering to prevent retreat turning into a rout. The country effectively had a one-party system by the end of the civil war, so the main possible arena for conflict was the party itself. Lenin had never tolerated much disagreement in the Bolshevik Party before the revolution, but in 1917 and the first years in power, he tolerated it willy-nilly on a number of issues – among others, whether or not to take power in October (Zinoviev and others had doubts); whether to sign the Brest-Litovsk Treaty with the Germans in 1918 (Bukharin and the 'left Communists' were against); and whether Tsarists officers ('bourgeois specialists') could be used, under appropriate control, in the Red Army during the civil war (Trotsky was for, Stalin against).

By the end of 1920, factional struggle had not just become established practice within the party but had also generated an issue of principle. A group called 'Democratic Centralists' advocated more democracy within the party, while Lenin thought there was already too much. If the Democratic

Centralists had won, the party might have become an umbrella for a range of organised factions seeking support for particular agendas, with outcomes decided by votes that all accepted as binding – but such pluralism went against the grain for most rank-and-file Bolsheviks, who wanted decisive rather than democratic leadership and tended to view disagreements at the top with disapproval. In any case, Lenin was not about to let this happen. At the Tenth Party Congress, he shamelessly mobilised his own faction – including Stalin and candidate Politburo member Molotov – to push through a resolution 'On party unity' that banned factions. That provided Lenin's group with a useful weapon to use against opponents, who could now be accused of violating the ban on factionalism. But it would be a mistake to jump to the conclusion that the resolution actually caused factions in the party to disappear. In fact, they flourished throughout the 1920s as never before – until Stalin put an end to them.

WHERE TO NOW?

The 1920s were often nostalgically represented in retrospect as a golden age of pluralism and permissiveness. But 'golden age' was not how it felt at the time; an age of anxiety was more like it. Workers were worried about unemployment. Peasants, especially the older ones, were baffled by the Bolsheviks' Westernised vocabulary and alien frame of reference: Who was Karlo-Mars? What was *levoliutsiia* (a mishearing of the equally incomprehensible *revoliutsiia*)? Why did young people from the towns call themselves *komsomoltsy* (Komsomol was the acronym for Communist Union of Youth) and

Anatoly Lunacharsky (on the right), the first People's Commissar of Enlightenment (1917–1929), with his secretary and brother-in-law Igor Sats (later one of the editors of *Novy Mir*) in the mid-1920s

mock the priests? If Lenin was the new Tsar, why didn't they call him that? Why did the Bolsheviks' 'women's departments' try to draw decent peasant and working-class women out of their proper sphere into public life, and why were men now able to throw over their wives and children in so-called 'postcard divorces'? Ordinary townspeople – the ones the Bolsheviks called 'petty-bourgeois philistines' – were apprehensive because they felt buffeted by barely understood political storms and were afraid of what the Bolsheviks might do next. The intelligentsia (later to become propagators of the 'golden age' myth) were annoyed, at the time, that the Bolsheviks called them 'bourgeois', ignored their pretensions to moral leadership and would not let them run institutions like universities and state theatres without political oversight. It was a time of great avant-garde vitality in the arts, but also of bitter artistic factionalism, the competing factions being constantly at one another's throats and denouncing one another to the authorities.

Party members were also full of anxiety. They worried about whether they could do the managerial jobs for which they were often ill prepared. They felt threatened by capitalist spies and subversion, foreign military attack, a revanche of the pernicious bourgeoisie and the influence of kulaks, priests, Nepmen and other 'class enemies'. They were fearful, too, of 'masking': that is, bourgeois pretending to be proletarian, and kulaks pretending to be poor peasants – a totally justified fear, insofar as the Bolsheviks' policies of favouring and rewarding proletarians and penalising the bourgeoisie led all sorts of people into such deceptions. They worried about exhaustion and poor health within the precious cohort of 'Old Bolsheviks', and disillusionment and suicide among the young. They dreaded a 'Thermidorian degeneration' of the party, such as had occurred in the wake of the French Revolutionary terror. Civil war veterans missed their wartime camaraderie. Komsomol enthusiasts, too young to have fought, loudly bemoaned the party's alleged loss of militant spirit.

Lenin, in his last years, developed worries of his own about whether the party had the competence and culture to carry out the enormous tasks it had taken upon itself. In some of his late writings, he could sound almost like a 1917 Menshevik deploring the 'prematurity' of the October Revolution. But he was a sick man in those years, effectively removed by illness from the magic circle of power, and this was surely a major contributing cause of his pessimism. Lenin was only fifty in 1920, but his health had been affected by the bullet wound he received in a 1918 assassination attempt, and in May 1922 he had a stroke. He tried to keep working, but then came a second stroke in December, ending his participation in political life. There was a third stroke in March 1923, and on 21 January 1924 he died.

In the twenty months of his illness, isolated with his wife in his dacha outside Moscow, his anxiety about Russia's backwardness and the party's low cultural level became almost an obsession. The passivity of the masses, Lenin feared, left Communists to do all the heavy lifting, but the Communists themselves were mainly poorly educated and consequently at the mercy of government bureaucrats (old-regime holdovers) with different values. 'If we take Moscow, with its 4700 Communists in responsible positions, and if we take that huge bureaucratic machine, that gigantic heap, we must ask: who is directing whom?', he commented almost despairingly in 1922.

In this period, Lenin also became strongly critical of the party's 'oligarchical' tendencies, meaning, in effect, its rule by a Politburo of which he was no longer an active member due to his illness. Some historians have interpreted these late writings as evidence of Lenin's conversion to participatory democracy and pluralism. The possibility of such an interpretation would have considerable importance for future framing of debate within the Soviet Communist Party, since it allowed a 'democratic' Lenin to be invoked (as he was in the post-Stalin period) as a kind of counter-Stalin – a champion of legality against oppressive and arbitrary state power. Whether it is an accurate representation of Lenin in real life is more doubtful. As a skilled dialectician, Lenin was always capable of switching abruptly from one side of an argument to the other. He certainly deeply resented being cut out of the Politburo loop on doctors' orders. However, he had never complained about a Politburo oligarchy when he was heading it, and even during his illness, he neither suggested that the ban on factions should be lifted nor that the increasingly moribund soviets should be encouraged to resume active participation in political life. What undoubtedly did resurface in Lenin's last years was a humanist concern for the enlightenment of the people via the provision of schools, literacy classes, reading rooms and libraries, something he and his wife – now his sole companion – had always shared.

THE SUCCESSION STRUGGLE

Even before his death, Lenin's illness precipitated a faction fight within the leadership – so much for the ban on factions! – that was waged for half a decade and ultimately resulted in Stalin's emergence as the new leader. It was not initially conceptualised as a leadership fight but as a struggle to retain Politburo unity. Initially, the perceived threat to that unity was Trotsky – a civil war hero, with a popular fame second only to Lenin, but a latecomer to the Bolshevik Party and, to those who had read their French Revolutionary history, the man most likely to emerge as a Bonaparte and hijack the revolution. Most of the rest of the Politburo, including Stalin, Zinoviev and Bukharin, joined ranks to close him out, and succeeded.

Lenin was not directly involved in these wrangles, but shortly after his second stroke he wrote a letter to the Central Committee – known to historians, though not to Lenin, as his 'Testament' – summing up the capacities of various senior party members, including Trotsky, Stalin, Zinoviev and Bukharin. Distributing faint praise and criticism more or less equally, this document in its original form neither endorsed nor disqualified any of the potential candidates for leadership. But a few days later, Lenin added a postscript on Stalin, saying that he was 'too rude' and lacked the qualities necessary to be the party's general secretary. This assessment was provoked by a quarrel between Krupskaya and Stalin. The Politburo had given Stalin the thankless task of seeing that the doctors' orders to keep newspapers and official papers from Lenin were followed, but Krupskaya, who thought it agitated the patient more to be kept in ignorance, disobeyed. When Lenin heard that Stalin had abused her on this account, he weighed in with an extraordinarily un-Bolshevik statement – a real reversion to the honour code of his youth – that he could have no dealings with a man who had insulted his wife.

Lenin's comments hurt Stalin personally – he is said to have fled Moscow and holed up alone in a dacha for several days after the letter was produced – and caused him considerable political embarrassment. But at the time they were made, Stalin was not perceived by anyone, except perhaps himself, as a plausible successor to Lenin. He was the colourless backroom man with a Georgian accent who, as general secretary, did the boring organisational work that other Politburo members had no time for. Even in the fight with Trotsky in 1923–1924, Stalin was just one of a Politburo group, the 'Central Committee majority', defending party unity from Trotsky's challenge. The group included Zinoviev, head of the Leningrad branch of the party and the Comintern, who probably thought of himself as its leader, and the popular but younger and somewhat lightweight Bukharin, who was editor of the party newspaper, *Pravda*, and would succeed Zinoviev as head of the Comintern in 1926.

The succession struggle was the basic issue underlying the factional conflicts of the 1920s, though it was not openly acknowledged as such, and the party, lacking a *Führerprinzip* or an office to go with it, formally had no individual leader to replace. But then Lenin died, and everything changed as a result of an outpouring of popular demand – taken up by some of the party leaders, but not originating from them – that he be essentially deified. 'Lenin lives' became the slogan of the day, and his followers were exhorted to carry out his legacy. To the horror of his atheist widow and many of his comrades, his body was embalmed and placed in a mausoleum next to the Kremlin. The Lenin cult had been well and truly launched and so, tacitly, had the assumption that the party required a leader (in Russian, *vozhd'*).

While succession was the major underlying issue in the faction fighting of the 1920s, there were also policy issues at stake. Of these, the overarching one was whether to go with aggressive policies that were popular in the party or conciliatory ones that appealed to the population. Picking fights with some alien group – Nepmen, kulaks, priests, 'bourgeois specialists', capitalist foreigners – and using state power to crush it was a good strategy for maintaining the party's sense of revolutionary identity and purpose. But making concessions to the population, particularly the peasantry, in order to win them over and make the regime more secure, was clearly the prudent course. It was the latter approach that prevailed for most of the 1920s.

The conflict with Trotsky started on issues of policy, not party leadership, while Lenin was still alive. The issues were the growth of bureaucratism within the party, a lack of consultation with the rank and file, and the excessive power of a small 'Old Bolshevik' elite, concerns close to those Lenin had expressed. The 'New Course' manifesto that Trotsky put out in 1923 was a call for generational change that initiated widespread discussion within the party. In the winter

Lenin Mausoleum: a 1950s view of Alexey Shchusev's granite constructivist monument from the 1920s, set in Red Square against the Kremlin wall

of 1923–1924, the selection of delegates for the upcoming Thirteenth Party Congress turned into something like a real election campaign in local party branches, with some delegates supporting Trotsky's theses, others those of the 'Democratic Centralists' (who had been raising the issue of party democracy since 1920) and still others the 'Central Committee majority' line of Zinoviev and Stalin – which won, but in the face of substantial dissent.

Trotsky's faction was then labelled an 'Opposition' to the 'Central Committee majority', as neat a piece of branding as Lenin's in 1903, when he called his minority faction of the Social Democratic Labour Party the 'Bolsheviks'. Zinoviev, Kamenev and Stalin were now the triumvirate in control, and in mid-1924, Zinoviev, with Politburo backing, launched a campaign, 'Face to the countryside', to bring more economic and cultural resources to the villages and convince the peasants that proletarian power was on their side. Bukharin took up the theme with a call to peasants to 'get rich', which was also an implicit plea to Communists to stop labelling any modern-minded, prosperous peasant a kulak exploiter. There was also a push to revitalise the soviets, once bastions of popular democracy but now languishing. For a few years, the practice of limiting candidates in soviet elections to those nominated by the local party was abandoned: with party and Komsomol organisations relaxing their control, locals were free to put forward their own candidates and vote more or less for whom they liked.

Thus there were democratic flickers in the mid-1920s, both within the party and the soviets. But the experiment with soviet democracy soon faded (too many villagers wanted to elect local authority figures whom the local party regarded as class enemies), and party democracy fared no better. After the comparatively close-run quasi-election of May 1924, Stalin, as head of the party secretariat, put more effort into stacking the congress by selecting Moscow-approved delegates in the regions. This was facilitated by the fact that the factions gained little traction in the party outside the capitals. Local Communists were inclined to put Politburo conflicts into the age-old Russian category of 'fighting among the boyars' and to view Oppositionists as privileged *frondeurs*.

Stalin's control over the appointments of regional party secretaries – who in turn were often sent as delegates from their regions to the party congresses that elected the Central Committee and ultimately the Politburo – established a 'circular flow of power' greatly to Stalin's advantage. But there was more to those regional party secretaries than simply playing the clients to Stalin's patron. They were 'little Stalins', surrounded by 'families' of their own political clients, without whom Moscow could not have governed the provinces. To be sure, there were recurrent scandals and occasional purges, but overall, the power of the first party secretary in his fiefdom, and as a lobbyist for it with Moscow, would be a constant for the whole life of the Soviet Union.

By the mid-1920s, with the economy back to semi-normal functioning after the disruption of the civil war, it was time to think more seriously about a fundamental party commitment: industrialisation. Everyone agreed on the necessity of rapid industrialisation to create the prerequisites for socialism, but opinion was divided on how rapid it should be and where the money for investment in thousands of new factories, mines, hydro-electric schemes and railways should come from. Some, including Trotsky at times, were in favour of the cautious use of foreign investors, despite Lenin's strictures on that issue, but it was unclear whether any foreign capitalists would want to invest, not to mention whether such a policy could be sold to the party as a whole. Five years earlier, it had been possible to hope that the whole issue of how to manage Russia's economic development would be made moot by the victory of revolution in the West, enabling Russia to join up with Germany and other more advanced economies. Now that hope was gone, and Stalin was only stating the obvious when he put forward the slogan 'Socialism in one country' – there was no other option on offer.

But if industrialisation had to be launched without foreign investment, that money had to be found somewhere in the domestic economy, and unfortunately most of those with money (the 'exploiters') had already been expropriated. 'Squeezing the peasants' – that is, making them pay more for the goods they bought from the town and giving them less for the goods they brought to market – looked like a good option to many. But it was scarcely compatible with the 'Face to the countryside' policies favoured by Zinoviev, and there was also the worry that too much pressure on the peasantry might precipitate revolts.

After a year or so, Stalin manoeuvred Zinoviev and Kamenev, the other two members of the anti-Trotsky triumvirate, into a new Opposition that, too late for any real political impact, joined forces with Trotsky's Opposition. As the dance of the factions became ever more complicated, it became harder to see which policies the various factions were identified with. Trotsky was generally a maximalist ('leftist'), pushing for the most ambitious and quickest plan of economic development. Bukharin, a radical on social questions in the early '20s, had swung around and become a 'rightist'. Stalin sometimes looked like a rightist and sometimes a leftist, recalling the contemporary joke that 'the party line never deviates', accompanied by hand gestures showing it veering first to the left, then the right.

Along with the cult of Lenin, a new pernicious cult was taking hold – that of the party and the correctness of its 'line'. 'The party is always right' had become the mantra, and before too long, respected Old Bolsheviks were being forced to make abject apologies for their Oppositionist views in front of jeering and whistling delegates at the annual party congresses. Krupskaya, who had joined the Zinoviev Opposition in 1925, was the rare exception who stood up to the heckling and declined to apologise, even mocking – as only Lenin's widow could have dared to do – the idea that the party could not err.

It was perhaps surprising that Stalin, part of the 1 per cent of party members who were Georgian as against the 72 per cent who were Russians, should have landed the leadership prize at the end of the 1920s. Although he spoke Russian with an accent, he increasingly identified as Russian. A great advantage, undoubtedly, was that his two main competitors – Trotsky and Zinoviev – were Jewish, and, as Trotsky himself acknowledged, a Jewish leader was a bridge too far for the general population of the country, and perhaps for the party's rank and file as well. If Bukharin, a genuine Russian, had been a better politician, he might have had a chance against Stalin, but by the time he made his move it was too late. The Jewish issue was not openly exploited by Stalin, but it almost certainly coloured the party debate on Stalin's 'Socialism in one country', in which Trotsky was painted into a corner as the internationalist. Of course internationalism was a core Leninist party policy. But the word was also taking on connotations as a marker for Jewishness.

The Bolsheviks were not averse to using terror against class enemies, and had done so freely during the civil war before pulling back somewhat during NEP. But they always expressed strong disapproval of allowing 'the revolution to eat its own children' (that is, using terror as a weapon against party opponents), as in the French Revolution. Under Lenin, those defeated in policy conflicts were not forced out of the party, and by common consent, the Cheka and its successor, the GPU, left the party leaders alone. That changed late in 1927, when leading Oppositionists were expelled from the party and those who refused to break with the Opposition were sent off into internal exile by the GPU. Trotsky's destination was Alma-Ata, on the Chinese border in Kazakhstan, although by a strange oversight he was allowed to take all his books and papers (which subsequently ended up in Harvard's Widener Library), and keep up an extensive correspondence with his followers exiled to different parts of the country. Two years later (February 1929), in an extraordinary break with party tradition, he was deported from the Soviet Union – his home country – as a traitor to the revolution. Eleven years after that, he would be murdered in Mexico by Stalin's assassin.

Trotsky, an arrogant man, always despised Stalin and was slow to see him as a real political threat. Stalin was neither an orator nor a theorist (two areas, highly valued in the party, in which Trotsky excelled), and having been educated in an Orthodox seminary in Georgia before dropping out to become a professional revolutionary, he was not even an intellectual in Trotsky's eyes. He was no cosmopolitan: instead of spending years in emigration, his revolutionary apprenticeship had been served in prison and internal exile. There were no towering achievements in his biography, such as heading

Dzerzhinsky Square (formerly Lubyanka) in Moscow, with a statue of Felix Dzerzhinsky by Yevgeny Vuchetich, erected in 1958. Secret police headquarters are partially visible on the right.

the Petersburg Soviet in 1905 or creating the Red Army from nothing in the civil war. Lenin's snub in the 'Testament' had been a substantial political setback. He was a 'grey blur' (to quote the memoirist Nikolai Sukhanov); a mere 'creature of the bureaucracy', as Trotsky would later claim; a 'crude man', as he admitted himself when apologising for his rudeness to Krupskaya during Lenin's illness. Trotsky scarcely even bothered to be polite to him, still less to those who supported him, a group that from the mid-1920s included several Politburo members, notably Molotov, ex-Red Cavalry man Klim Voroshilov and Kaganovich, a candidate member of the Politburo who was first secretary of the party in Ukraine.

Trotsky's contempt – generally echoed, until the Soviet archives opened in the 1990s, by historians – was woefully off the mark. Stalin was not a mediocrity, he was not stupid and he was nobody's creature. If others played a more stellar part in the policy debates of the 1920s, it was Stalin who came to a simple conclusion about the way forward. Lenin had led the party to victory in the political revolution of October, but the economic revolution – crucial in Marxist terms – was still to come. Stalin would be the man to lead it.

3

STALINISM

IF THE SOVIET UNION STILL REQUIRED a second revolution, an economic one, how was it to be carried out? Obviously not by people spontaneously coming out onto the streets, as in 1917. This revolution needed to be planned (after all, its purpose was to realise the idea of centralised economic planning) and directed from Moscow. Historians have often called it a 'revolution from above', stressing the 'from above' aspect. That is quite accurate, as long as the 'revolution' part is not overlooked. The extraordinary thing about Stalin's economic-transformation program is that it was, in fact, carried out by quasi-revolutionary means – to achieve its aims, Stalin mobilised the party and its supporters for violence against other parts of the population.

It might seem odd to present a program of planned, state-sponsored industrialisation as if it were a revolutionary war against 'class enemies' and 'foreign interventionists'. But Stalin was, after all, a revolutionary: violence and the stirring up of class resentments were things he knew how to do.

Vera Mukhina's iconic statue, *Worker and Collective Farm Woman*, was first shown in the Soviet pavilion at the International Exhibition in Paris in 1937.

The party knew how to do them as well. In terms of economic rationality, the method was very wasteful, but given the militant mindset of the party and its civil war formation, it had its own political rationality.

The 'Great Break' of 1929–1932, as Stalin himself called it, had three aspects. The first was forced-pace industrialisation, carried out according to a Five-Year Plan worked out by the state planning agency; the second was agricultural collectivisation; and the third was 'cultural revolution', a term the Soviets invented long before its replay in the 1960s by the Chinese Communists. The violence surrounding all three new aspects of the program served to intimidate the non-Communist population and cow it into submission. But its purpose was also to rally Stalin's own troops – Communists, young Communists, 'conscious' urban workers – by letting them do what at this point they still really wanted to do, which was to pick fights with people they considered their enemies.

As is common at moments of domestic crisis, an alleged foreign threat was invoked as a stimulus to action. Although there was no real evidence that the (admittedly hostile) Western capitalist powers were preparing any immediate military operations against the Soviet Union, the Soviet press had for months been playing up a war scare. The cultural revolution – conceptualised as a movement to overthrow 'bourgeois dominance' in the cultural sphere – tied in with this, since it was launched early in 1928 with dramatically publicised show trials of engineers ('bourgeois specialists') on charges of industrial sabotage and spying for foreign intelligence agencies. This started a witch-hunt in the factories against 'wrecker' engineers, whose privileged social status workers often resented.

It was industrialisation, not agricultural collectivisation, that was at the centre of the economic agenda of Stalin's revolution. Collectivisation was actually a secondary objective that, given predictable peasant resistance, might prudently have been left until a later date. But it was class-war imperatives, not prudence, that won arguments in the Soviet Communist Party in 1928. Not for the first time, peasants and the Soviet government were engaged in a tussle about prices for agricultural goods. The state could have raised its procurement prices, but conventional wisdom among the economists held that the only way to finance industrialisation was to 'squeeze' the peasantry. In a brief, rare foray outside the capital, Stalin went to Siberia to look at the situation for himself.

He came back with the news that 'kulaks' were holding back grain from the market, trying to drive the prices up, and that this amounted to political sabotage. New punishments for 'hoarding' were introduced; more peasant resistance ensued. The program of all-out collectivisation launched in the winter of 1929 was meant to solve the problem once and for all by making the newly formed collective farms the sole legal marketer of grain and the state their only customer. The kulak problem would also be solved definitively by kicking the kulaks out of the village.

Meanwhile, in the towns, another class enemy was under siege in a campaign to de-privatise the urban economy. With the help of the GPU, Nepmen and small traders and manufacturers were put out of business (and often into prison as well). This was another rash and ill-thought-out policy that required the state to set up its own retail network in a hurry, almost without advance planning. The outcome was shortages, rationing (another measure that conveyed wartime crisis to the population) and their corollary, rapid growth of the black market.

COLLECTIVISATION AND CULTURAL REVOLUTION
Collectivisation was supposed to be a voluntary process. But in the villages there were few signs of any spontaneous desire to collectivise, and coercion was built into the fabric of the program via a parallel process called 'dekulakisation', which meant that the land and dwellings of people labelled kulaks were seized and the 'kulaks' themselves were deported by the GPU and resettled in distant parts of the Soviet Union. The slogan was 'liquidation of kulaks as a class', but as few old-style

kulaks exploiting the labour of poor peasants remained in the villages (partly as a result of efforts to curb such practices in the 1920s), any unpopular figure in the village could be so labelled and duly punished. Brigades of Communists and urban volunteers were sent out to the villages to organise collectivisation, which essentially meant persuading peasants to sign up for the *kolkhoz* (collective farm) under the implicit threat of being expelled from the village as kulaks if they did not. On signing up, peasants were required to hand over their horses to plough the collective fields that would now be consolidated out of the traditional strips of individual households; sometimes the collectivisers took other animals as well.

For all the contemporary excitement about planning, collectivisation was launched virtually without preparation; the process was largely made up on the fly. No clear instructions were given either to collectivisers or to the peasants, and necessary facilities such as collective stables had not been ordered. When things went wrong, Stalin blamed overzealous local officials. Soviet propaganda represented collectivisation as a move from small- to large-scale farming and from age-old manual techniques to modern mechanised ones. But there were not enough tractors and combine harvesters to go round, and the peasants did not know how to use them. In addition, despite all the publicity given to enormous new collective farms with names like 'Giant', it proved too hard as a general rule to set up functioning agricultural units larger than the existing villages, so smaller farms were (quietly) settled for.

Collectivisation was enforced nationwide, but there were regional variations. In Kazakhstan, where the native herding population was still largely nomadic, it was a corollary of compulsory sedentarisation, provoking mass resistance and flight across the border into China. Georgia, with its agricultural focus on fruit, wine and technical crops, rather than grain, got a milder version than the norm, thanks to the protective efforts of local Communist leaders, including Lavrenty Beria. In areas with ethnically mixed populations, the majority ethnic group sometimes tried to pin the kulak label on a comparatively prosperous minority group such as German farmers. More ethnic tensions were created by dumping deported Russian and Ukrainian kulaks in such places as Kazakhstan.

Five to six million peasants, constituting about 4 per cent of all peasant households, were victims of dekulakisation (including those who fled to the towns under threat of expropriation). Of the two million deported outside their own regions, the majority were resettled in uncultivated rural areas and a substantial minority sent to work on new industrial construction sites. There were no large-scale revolts in European Russia: the extraordinary measure of out-of-the-blue terror proved a sufficient deterrent for most peasants; anger and passive resistance, however, were widespread. Peasants slaughtered their livestock rather than handing them over, and hid grain to avoid delivering their procurements quotas. Rumours circulated that collectivisation was the coming of Antichrist, and that the collectivisers were about to cut off the women's hair and institute communal marriage. In a popular form of resistance, groups of peasant women (less likely than men to be arrested) followed the collectivisers round the village, demonstratively weeping and singing hymns.

One of the most remarkable aspects of collectivisation was the parallel campaign against priests and the church in the Russian and Ukrainian countryside, and against Buddhism and Islam in other regions of the country. This clearly indicates that 'class war' violence was an integral part of the process, since anyone seriously hoping to persuade peasants to change their traditional farming and marketing habits would surely not add insult to injury by going after the local church or mosque. But that is just what urban brigades of Komsomols did when they came in to 'collectivise', gleefully vandalising churches, digging up graveyards and dancing around with skeletons, and taking down the church bells 'as scrap metal for industrialisation'. Meanwhile, the GPU was quietly arresting priests and deporting them to the interior along with the 'kulaks'. How deep Russian peasants' Christian faith was before this assault on the church is debatable, but persecution certainly reinforced it. As for the urban collectivisers, some were sorry for the peasants, but many believed in the threat from class enemies in the countryside, especially when angry peasants took pot shots at them or stealthily waylaid them at night and threw them into the river. It was a baptism by fire (though not too much fire) that joined the heroic legends of civil-war struggle in Communist mythology.

In the cities and towns, cultural revolution ranged from the carnivalesque to the curricular. The Soviet Komsomols never went quite as far as the Chinese Red Guards, who in their later Cultural Revolution would parade actual live victims through the streets in dunces' caps, but the Komsomols also had their parades where effigies of priests and

Nepmen were mocked and sometimes burnt. 'Light cavalry' brigades invaded government offices, scattering files around and accusing the employees of being 'bureaucrats'. In Central Asia, the unveiling of women became more coercive and widespread. University students held meetings to denounce 'bourgeois' professors, who then had to publicly confess their political sins and promise to introduce Marxist texts into their syllabi. The most egregious actions of cultural revolutionaries sometimes earned rebukes from party leaders, but generally it was seen as 'excess' in a good cause – that of overthrowing tradition and dislodging the bourgeoisie from its position of cultural dominance. The enthusiasm of young Communists for the job was unmistakable: as one contemporary observer put it, they had been itching to be 'unleashed'.

A less anarchic aspect of cultural revolution was the drive for affirmative action (to use an anachronistic term) on behalf of workers, poor peasants and 'backwards' ethnic groups that took high priority in the late 1920s. Women were on the affirmative action list too, but with much lower priority in this period, which also saw the disbanding of the Central Committee's women's department. Affirmative action meant both direct promotion into managerial jobs and preferential admission to higher and technical education, the latter being accompanied, in good cultural revolutionary style (but not without anguish on the part of the educational authorities), by purging existing students who came from bourgeois, kulak and clerical families. Affirmative action was something new on the international scene in 1930; there was not even a contemporary English-language term to describe it.

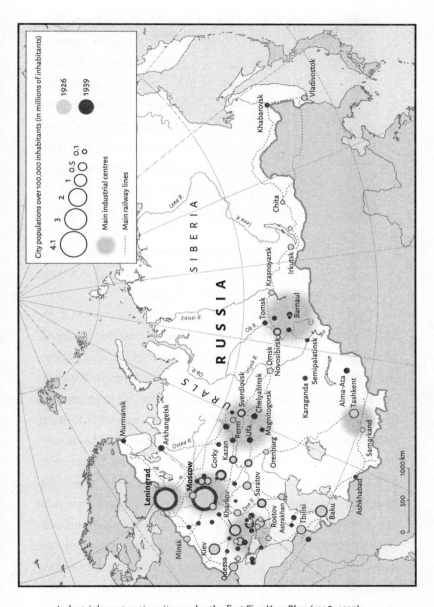

Industrial construction sites under the first Five-Year Plan (1928–1932)

Multiculturalism in the 1930s: Georgian Joseph Stalin and Russian
Klim Voroshilov in Central Asian robes presented to them by prize-
winning collective farmers of Turkmenistan and Tajikistan in 1936.
Sergo Ordzhonikidze, in military jacket, is on the right.

Marxist theorists might disdain the program, since workers
should not wish to leave their class, but working-class, peasant and non-Russian families appreciated the opportunity for
advancement. Future national leaders Nikita Khrushchev and
Leonid Brezhnev, along with a raft of native-son leaders in the
republics, were among the grateful beneficiaries.

INDUSTRIALISATION

The first Five-Year Plan was the earliest effort in national
economic planning for the Soviet Union (and, as Soviet propagandists reiterated, for the world), focusing on rapid development of heavy industry, particularly mining, metallurgy
and machine-building. The ambitious plan was to double
the state's investment in industry over the past five years and

achieve a tripling of output from the prewar level. The problem of where to find the capital investment was never satisfactorily solved: in the short run, collectivising the peasants did not prove an effective method of 'squeezing', since the expenses were greater than anticipated and the returns slower to come through. An increase in state vodka production (needed, as Stalin wrote to Molotov in 1930, to pay for military expansion) helped fill the gap, as did a sharp, unplanned drop in the standard of living in the towns.

Not having much capital to throw at the problem, the Soviet state threw cheap labour. Women joining the workforce for the first time – the main focus of women's emancipation in this period – were one important source, with almost ten million women entering paid employment in the course of the 1930s; the urban unemployed constituted another reserve. But the primary labour source tapped was the peasantry, with kulak deportation a major contributor to this process, and the GPU, together with Gulag's growing network of labour camps, becoming a key industrial supplier. In addition, millions of young peasants left the villages for the towns during collectivisation, some fleeing dekulakisation or the kolkhoz and others simply seeking opportunity now that jobs in the towns had opened up. In the years of the first Five-Year Plan, one peasant left the village and became a wage-earner for every three who stayed and became kolkhozniks. An extraordinary twelve million moved permanently from village to town in the period of 1928–1932 alone.

Had anyone had the gall to point it out, collectivisation was serving the same function in the Soviet Union as the enclosure movement in eighteenth- and nineteenth-century England, which had ruthlessly driven farmers off the land, thus providing the labour force for the industrial revolution, as Marx had noted. To what degree this result was anticipated and formed part of the regime's collectivisation strategy is unclear. Stalin, at any rate, was not telling. In a strikingly mendacious speech celebrating the success of collectivisation in abolishing rural poverty, he claimed – in a year when the Soviet urban population increased by four million – that because of the attractions of the kolkhoz, the traditional 'peasant flight' from village to town had become a thing of the past.

In drafting the first Five-Year Plan and its successors, the big arguments were about what new plants, railways and hydro-electric schemes the state should build, and where to build them. This had some unacknowledged resemblance to pork-barrel politics in the West. One of the most heated and long-running debates was about whether to focus development on Ukraine, which had more modern infrastructure but was uncomfortably close to the western border, or in the Urals, less modern in its industrial base but geographically more secure. A long-standing assumption among Soviet planners and politicians was that the country's industrially less-developed regions, such as Siberia, Central Asia and the Caucasus, should have priority. But there were competing imperatives, including security ones: with the build-up of the country's defence capability as one of the major objectives of the first Five-Year Plan, Stalin was inclined to favour the Russian/Ukrainian heartland over non-Slavic regions as a location for defence-related plants. These choices were for the Politburo to make, however, not Stalin alone, and the decision process involved heavy and continuous lobbying from the republics and regions for their favourite projects. Such lobbying – and, more generally, the representation of regional interests in Moscow – became a key task of republican and regional first secretaries. A number of Politburo members also had their own territories to defend at budget time, none more (or more successfully) than the People's Commissar for Heavy Industry, Stalin's fellow Georgian, Sergo Ordzhonikidze.

Magnitogorsk, the great metallurgical complex built in the Urals in the middle of nowhere, was a quintessential construction project of the first Five-Year Plan, embodying many of its contradictions. Heavily dependent on the labour of convicts and deported kulaks under GPU guard, with 'wrecker' engineers removed from more salubrious regions working alongside newly

Happy life on the collective farm (1931), as depicted in F.F. Kondratov's poster for the spectacle *Flax* staged at Moscow's Theatre of Worker Youth

trained Communists, Magnitogorsk was also a mecca for young Komsomol volunteers, fired up with a sense of fighting against the odds to 'conquer nature' and build Soviet industry in the empty steppe. It was a classic frontier town, full of hardship but also plenty of adventure and comradeship, a place where people's origins could often be forgotten, and an erstwhile kulak's son could become a Stakhanovite (super-achieving) worker and then join the Komsomol. 'New Soviet man' was being forged here, if not exactly in the form envisaged in the blueprints.

A distinctive culture of boasting emerged in the Soviet press, which every day proclaimed the country's 'achievements' (a key word of the 1930s) in the building of socialism: so many tons of iron ore mined, so many blast furnaces put into operation, so many miles of railway track laid, so many kilowatt-hours of electricity produced by the new hydroelectric plants. There were 'no fortresses that Bolsheviks could not storm', Stalin said, using one of the military metaphors that had become ubiquitous. But many 'ambushes' and 'tactical retreats' occurred along the way. Soviet planning, at this point, meant deciding priorities among competing projects and setting output targets and urging enterprises to 'overfulfil' them – not working out in detail where a particular tractor factory would get the rubber for its tires. Consequently, industrial enterprises had an informal army of 'agents' paid out of plant directors' slush funds to search out the necessary supplies and make sure it was dispatched in their direction.

With shortages of food and consumer goods even more critical than that of industrial raw materials, Soviet citizens honed similar skills to the best of their ability. 'It is better to have a hundred friends than a hundred rubles,' the Soviet saying went; access to goods through 'connections' was the key, while having the money to pay for them was secondary. This applied as much to the worker in a shoe factory who could slip a pair of galoshes to a friend from the kolkhoz in exchange for potatoes, as to a district party secretary or an academician. 'Whom do you go to?' the wife of police chief Nikolai Ezhov asked the wife of the poet Osip Mandelstam when they chanced to meet at an elite resort. She meant: 'Who is your patron?' High-minded Nadezhda did not at first understand the question, but her husband did, explaining: 'We go to Nikolai Bukharin.'

RESULTS

The first two Five-Year Plans did produce industrial break-through, though at tremendous cost and with massive wast-age. Soviet figures claimed a doubling on gross industrial production between 1928 and 1932 and a further doubling in the next Five-Year Plan period, for an average annual growth rate of almost 17 per cent for the period of 1928–1940. Western analysts (and revisionist Soviet economists of the 1980s) put that annual growth rate closer to 10 per cent, but even that was quite impressive. Some production indices like oil, coal, lorries and tractors already showed steep rises by the end of the first Five-Year Plan. But much of the effort of the first plan went into creating plants producing such resources as pig iron and rolled steel, and these were not functional until the mid-1930s. The only consumer item whose production went up was vodka, which by the mid-1930s was supplying up to a fifth of total state revenues.

Full employment was basically achieved during the first Five-Year Plan, and unemployment disappeared from the Soviet repertoire of social problems for the next sixty years. But the diversion of funds to heavy industry meant that social-welfare programs were chronically underfunded, generally available only to urban wage and salary earners and, in practice, often restricted to privileged groups such as workers in key industries.

In terms of the geographical distribution of industrial production, the Urals, Siberia and Central Asia had increased their share substantially (though in the case of Central Asia from a very low base). The Soviet Union was still a long way behind its Western capitalist competitors but had pulled level with Japan. It is possible, as some economists have argued, that similar results could have been achieved less wastefully by more moderate policies – but perhaps only in a country whose political culture embraced moderation.

The big failure was collectivisation, which set back Soviet agriculture for decades, alienated the peasantry and made food shortages endemic in the towns. After Stalin's death, Soviet politicians would say that it was not collectivisation itself but its 'excesses' that were to blame. But the excesses were part of the package. In the short term, the high procurements targets imposed on the collective farms hit hardest in the major grain-growing regions of the country. The present-day Ukrainian government claims this famine, known in Ukraine as 'Holodomor', was the result of a conscious plan on Stalin's part to kill Ukrainians; however, the results were equally devastating in southern Russia and Kazakhstan. It seems unlikely that Stalin actually wanted to kill peasants;

rather, he wanted the state to take the greatest possible amount of grain out of the villages consistent with its peasant producers surviving until the spring sowing. The trouble was that nobody knew what that amount was, and Stalin certainly pushed local officials to go for the maximum and refused to listen when told that the peasants had no more hidden reserves. A bizarre rhetoric about peasants 'acting a famine' and 'pretending to be ruined' entered Soviet discourse, and by the time Stalin was finally convinced that they were not pretending but actually dying, it was too late. Entry to the towns had to be blocked against peasants fleeing starvation in the winter of 1932–1933, and come spring, grain had to be sent out from state reserves for the sowing. Famine deaths (unadmitted by the Soviets until decades later) have been calculated at upwards of five million. The famine left deep scars, but remained publicly unmentionable for half a century until, during perestroika, Ukrainian party secretary Volodymyr Shcherbytsky broke silence on the seventieth anniversary of the founding of the Ukrainian Soviet republic.

'CONGRESS OF VICTORS'

Contrary to custom, which dictated that annual national party congresses be held to discuss important policies and elect the Central Committee and Politburo, none occurred between 1930 and 1934. In 1930, the Sixteenth Party Congress had seen the relatively easy defeat of a 'right' faction in the party led by Bukharin and Alexei Rykov, Lenin's successor at the head of the government, which advocated a more moderate approach to collectivisation and industrialisation. This was the last open faction in the party, signifying the long-delayed implementation of Lenin's 1921 ban on factions. Any subsequent factional organisation had to be small-scale and conspiratorial, and was quickly nipped in the bud. A growing Stalin cult emerged around this same time, which involved crediting all government initiatives to Stalin personally and thanking him profusely for everything from a happy childhood to local over-fulfilment of the cotton plan. Like Lenin, although perhaps less sincerely, Stalin publicly dismissed the cult, attributing it to the simplicity of the masses, who were used to having a Tsar, and presented himself to foreign interviewers as a modest, unpretentious man.

The Seventeenth Party Congress, representing a party whose membership was now approaching two million, styled itself as 'the Congress of Victors'. But it was a hard-won victory, if such it could be called with the famine scarcely over, and there must have been many in the party elite who privately blamed Stalin for the agricultural problems that followed collectivisation. Always suspicious, Stalin's temperament had been soured by the suicide of his wife at the end of 1932. Omnipresent tributes to the 'great leader and teacher' were not going to convince him that everyone loved him. From his perspective, there had to be discontent out there – the question was exactly where, so that it could be found and rooted out. The tools to do this existed, the powers and jurisdiction of the security organs (renamed NKVD in 1934) having been greatly expanded by the campaigns against kulaks and Nepmen and the growth of Gulag.

Now that the 'war' had been won, Stalin and the party leadership energetically promoted the idea of a return to

Stalin at ease with close associates – Vyacheslav Molotov and Valerian Kuibyshev, second and third from left; Sergo Ordzhonikidze and probably a blurred Sergei Kirov in front; Dimitrov and Stalin on sofa; Klim Voroshilov, far right, behind Stalin – in 1934

normality. Of course, it was a new normal, with villages collectivised, smokestack industry spreading across the country, towns springing up from nothing, an urban workforce full of yesterday's peasants, an increased police presence and more terror still a looming possibility. Stalin's new slogan, 'Life has become better, comrades; life has become more cheerful', may have substituted the wish for the fact, but at least it offered an encouraging statement of intent. Rationing had been lifted and there were goods – for a price – in new 'commercial' state stores. Peasant households were allowed to grow non-grain crops on their private plots and own one cow (but still not a horse). Christmas trees, previously condemned as a bourgeois relic, were allowed back; wedding rings, ditto, reappeared for sale. Arrested engineers were quietly released, many simply returning to their old jobs. Students were sent back to their classes and had be polite to their professors again. Trade unions were encouraged to rethink their function, from their old role of protecting labour against management to a new one as providers and distributors of worker perks such as vacations and rest homes; they could even become managers of football teams.

In the memory of many people, the 1930s was a wonderful and exciting time to grow up – with the prospect of adventure (going off to 'conquer nature' and 'build socialism' in distant regions) and a sense of collective purpose that elevated one's own life from triviality. This sense of purpose and disdain for triviality was meant to be mirrored in literature and the arts – writers were now labelled 'engineers of the human soul'. 'Socialist realism' was the recommended method: it meant the ability to see the lineaments of the radiant future through the often messy and chaotic present, which translated stylistically into the use of traditional forms easily appreciated by a mass audience and the avoidance of avant-garde quirkiness. For creative artists, and the intelligentsia generally, there were pluses and minuses in the new post-cultural-revolutionary norm. Admonitory instructions on how to write and paint were a minus, but on the plus side was generous remuneration for what you wrote and painted, along with privileges and social status unknown since the Revolution. As of the mid-1930s, it seemed like more carrot than stick. Stalin had lent his personal prestige to the elevation of high culture and education, something that was to remain characteristic of the Soviet Union until the end.

There were even signs of political relaxation. A new Constitution of the USSR announced in 1936 that it was time to stop fighting 'class enemies', since the enemy classes had been liquidated and the classes that remained were 'non-antagonistic'. This was a dubious proposition in Marxist theory but otherwise a reassuring message. In addition, the Constitution guaranteed all the basic freedoms, including those such as freedom of speech and assembly that definitely did not exist in the Soviet Union at that point. Stalin put a lot of personal time and effort into drafting this document, and from its prominence in his personal archive, one must assume he was proud of the results.

Many have seen the 'Stalin' Constitution as a cynical propaganda ploy to deceive the West, but it was in fact directed at least as strongly towards a *Soviet* audience. In a new approach to gauging public opinion (pioneered the previous year on a draft law banning abortion, which was widely disapproved of outside the urban elite), the draft Constitution had been made the subject of a much-publicised 'national conversation' in which Soviet citizens were urged to volunteer their opinions on clauses of the document, and large numbers of them did so.

In line with the new Constitution, it was also announced that multiple candidates could be nominated in upcoming soviet elections, an attempt similar to that made in the mid-1920s to 'revitalise soviet democracy'. That mid-1920s experiment had fizzled because too many 'enemies' had been nominated. It remained to be seen if the replay would meet the same fate.

In parallel with relaxation at home was the Popular Front in the Moscow-directed international communist movement. For much of the 1920s, the Comintern had spent its energies fighting European social democrats, but the Nazis' coming to power in Germany in 1933 showed the folly of that, and the Popular Front of 1935 (a coalition of communist, socialist and radical parties against fascism) was the belated result.

Diplomatically, too, the Soviet Union took a more moderate and conciliatory course in the 1930s, joining the League of Nations and re-establishing diplomatic relations with the United States for the first time since the Revolution. Foreign Minister Maxim Litvinov did his best to further an anti-fascist coalition with the Western democracies, although residual suspicions on both sides made this uphill work.

THE GREAT PURGES

If impulses towards relaxation could be seen in many areas in the mid-1930s, there were also countervailing tendencies increasing political tension. One came from the international situation. The Soviet Union had called wolf on the threat of war before, but with the rise of Nazi Germany in central Europe, a new power that was strongly anti-communist and anti-Soviet, and bent on expansion towards the east, that threat had become real, putting the idea of any real return to normalcy in jeopardy. The second was domestic, arising out of the murder of Politburo member and Leningrad party leader Sergei Kirov by a disgruntled former Komsomol member in December 1934. The murderer was immediately apprehended, but speculation swirled – as in the wake of President

Kennedy's assassination in the United States in the 1960s – that someone had put him up to it.

Stalin has often been suspected in the West, and Nikita Khrushchev even hinted at his possible involvement in his 1956 'Secret Speech', but no evidence to confirm this ever turned up from the archives. Stalin himself pointed the finger at the defeated Opposition, with the result that Zinoviev and Kamenev were arrested on suspicion of conspiracy. For good measure, 'class enemies' – the usual suspects in the Soviet Union – were deported en masse from Leningrad to the hinterland by the secret police. More class enemies (female librarians of noble birth, who Stalin thought might have been planning to poison the party leaders) were found in the Kremlin administration, for which its head – Georgian Avel Enukidze, an old friend of Stalin's – was fired and subsequently arrested.

Enukidze was one of those who, as Stalin put it, mistakenly thought that in light of the great victory of the first Five-Year Plan, they could 'now afford to rest, to take a nap'. The call for vigilance was an increasingly intrusive background to the 'return to normality' policies of the mid-1930s. In June 1935, Zinoviev and Kamenev were tried for Kirov's murder, but the outcome was inconclusive; a year later, they were tried again, to maximum publicity in the first of the so-called Moscow show trials, and sentenced to death for involvement in the murder and other terrorist plots.

One of the party's periodic membership reviews was underway, resulting in so many expulsions for various derelictions, including sympathy with the Opposition, that in some

LIFE IN COMMUNAL APARTMENTS

Communal apartments (*kommunalki*) were first established partly in a spirit of 'class revenge' on the bourgeois families who before the revolution were their sole residents, but they became a core Soviet urban institution for decades because of shortage of housing. One room per family was the norm (including for the dispossessed bourgeois, formerly sole occupier), with kitchen, bathroom and corridor shared. But single people might be allocated only a 'corner' in the common area, sometimes even the window-

less space under the stairs. The endless quarrels and feuds over kitchen space, stolen utensils, noise and other annoyances became legendary. Divorce, with the couples often forced to continue living in the same apartment, was a nightmare. Neighbours denounced each other as 'speculators' (black-marketeers) and 'class aliens', sometimes out of spite but sometimes in the hope of provoking an arrest that would free up living space. Many *kommunalki* had their 'madwoman'; almost all had their drunk (in *Common Places*, Svetlana Boym memorably describes the urine of their *kommunalka's* drunk trickling under the door as her intelligentsia family entertained, for the first time, a foreign visitor). But children, including Svetlana, often remembered their array of communal 'aunts' and 'uncles' fondly; and in post-Soviet times. the *kommunalka* itself became the subject of a popular nostalgic post-Soviet TV series, *The Old Apartment*.

VIGNETTES OF THE GREAT PURGE

Nikolai Ezhov conferring with Joseph Stalin

Nikolai Ezhov, head of the NKVD, was 'a flame, burning the serpents' nests', wrote the Kazakh bard Dzhambul at the height of the Great Purges. Some ordinary citizens responded to the drama of serpent-hunting with enthusiasm. 'There can be no mercy for enemies of the Soviet people,' a peasant wrote, denouncing the bosses of his *kolkhoz*. Another concerned citizen sensed a counter-revolutionary signal when, on the day Zinoviev and Kamenev were executed as enemies of the people, Radio Moscow played Chopin's *Funeral March*. 'You look at a man and suddenly he turns into a swindler or a traitor before your very eyes,' wrote a diarist, evoking the climate of paranoia and suspicion. Anyone could be unmasked as a serpent, so at night people lay sleepless, waiting for the knock on the door. Relatives still at liberty queued up to send parcels to prisoners and wrote desperate letters to the authorities trying to save them. A man whose wife had been arrested as a 'spy' wrote to Molotov that she could not possibly be guilty, because, unlike him, she couldn't hide anything – it immediately showed on her face. Some people got lucky, and were assigned the apartments of those arrested – one such apartment in Leningrad came 'not only fully furnished, it actually had dishes, linen, dresses, and even playing cards,' exactly as it was when the owners were taken away. The new tenant didn't feel bad about it: 'They weren't arrested because of us, after all.'

regions, as of early 1937, there were more *former* members of the Communist Party than there were current members – a nice illustration of the paradox that the capacity of Stalin's regime to attract enthusiastic support was equalled only by its ability to turn supporters into (real or imagined) enemies. All of these ex-Communists were supposed to be registered on local blacklists and kept under observation.

Another paradox emerged when the 'democratic' tendency in the electoral policy of the mid-1930s took a repressive turn. As political tensions grew, it became less and less acceptable for local party branches to allow nomination of 'dubious' candidates. With no formal announcement, the soviet elections that were held at the end of 1937 turned out to follow the old single-candidate procedures. A parallel democratic

'On Vigilance', a 1937 cartoon of the Great Purges era by Iu Ganf. Citizens were urged to unmask hidden enemies of the people.

experiment in the party turned out, probably contrary to the origin intention, to be almost purely intimidatory when it was implemented in the spring of 1937. This was bad timing, coming in the wake of the second Moscow show trial of former Oppositionists and the call of the February–March Central Committee plenum for vigilance against enemies, including those with responsible party positions. With all party officers up for re-election and no lists of approved candidates being supplied by party branches, the obligatory pre-election meetings became sites of escalating denunciations and almost unbearable tension, as nobody knew whom it was safe to nominate. At one factory in provincial Russia, eight hundred members of the factory party organisation attended meetings *every evening for more than a month* before they managed to come up with a new party committee.

The process of terror we call 'the Great Purges', often obliquely referred to by Soviet citizens as '1937', was unequivocally launched early that year at the Central Committee plenum, which raised the spectre of sabotage of industry by its Communist leaders, and corruption and betrayal on the part of republican and regional party secretaries. Stalin was undoubtedly the initiator of this new terror, although at the plenum he had Molotov give the opening report. The second Moscow show trial, held the previous month in a blaze of national publicity, provided a dramatic backdrop. Defendants, including Ordzhonikidze's deputy at the People's Commissariat of Heavy Industry, were accused of wrecking, terrorism, espionage and treason, and all confessed before being sentenced to death and immediately executed. 'Shoot the mad dogs!' was the much-quoted cry of prosecutor Andrei Vyshin-sky. It was echoed in meetings of indignation throughout the country.

Ordzhonikidze fought hard but unavailingly in the last months of 1936 to get his deputy off the list of defendants in the upcoming show trial, and then committed suicide rather than see the cohort of Soviet industrialists he had nurtured destroyed. The industrial leaders, often accused of 'wrecking' and blamed for industrial accidents, were among the first in the firing line, along with republican and regional party sec-retaries (many of whom were also members of the party's Central Committee), who were accused of dictatorial meth-ods, abuse of power in their republics and regions, and nep-otism. In other words, they were accused of doing their jobs according to the implicit job descriptions that had developed in the 1930s. Where the republican leaders were nationals of the republics they led, as was the case in Ukraine, Uzbekistan, Armenia, Georgia and the Tatar Autonomous Republic, they were also accused of 'bourgeois nationalism'. Their extensive patronage networks enabled the process to snowball, ulti-mately bringing down entire republican and regional lead-erships. In Turkmenistan, the carnage was so great that the local party was left for months without a Central Committee.

The purge spread to the army in June 1937, when Marshal Mikhail Tukhachevsky and virtually all the top military com-mand (except for Politburo member Klim Voroshilov) were convicted in a closed court martial of conspiracy with the Germans and summarily executed. The officers ('Judases who have been bought by the fascists') were knocked off without lifting a finger to save themselves, let alone trying to get rid of Stalin – one of several examples in Soviet history of the army dog that failed to bark.

Arrests throughout the elite continued through 1937, fuelled by a steady stream of opportunistic denunciations against bosses, fellow workers and neighbours flowing in to the authorities. Even Politburo members were not exempt from the fear of a midnight knock on the door (although most in fact survived), and in a suspension of the normal rules of the game, they were unable to save clients or even family members from arrest. Prominent members of the intelligentsia fell victim to the purge, often in the wake of the disgrace of a political patron. Tramps, religious sectarians and habitual criminals were picked up in the interests of public order. Ethnic groups such as Poles, Finns and Germans who could be suspected of loyalty to an outside power were targeted, and those living near the border were deported en masse to distant areas of the Soviet Union.

As the terror showed signs of flagging in 1938, a third Moscow show trial featuring Bukharin and former GPU chief Genrikh Yagoda was held. As before, the defendants all publicly confessed, an act interpreted by ex-Communist Arthur Koestler in his novel *Darkness at Noon* as a last service to the party by these dedicated Bolsheviks. Perhaps, but it was also their last chance for public utterance, and it seems both men attempted to combine the required confession with an implicit counter-narrative contradicting it. ('If I had been a spy,' Yagoda said, 'dozens of countries could have closed down their intelligence services.')

Like medieval witch-hunts, the Great Purges acquired their own deadly momentum in a population already conditioned to violence and suspicion. Ending it by fiat from the top was likely to be a much tricker enterprise than starting it had been. Stalin went at it gradually, letting the purge wind down through 1938 before symbolically ending it by calling in Lavrenty Beria as new police chief to purge the purgers – the secret police itself, and its former head, Nikolai Ezhov. In another 'dog that failed to bark' episode, the secret police offered no resistance to their own destruction. Ezhov, visibly in disfavour since April 1938, sat passively for more than six months until the axe finally fell, drinking steadily to pass the time.

Bringing the purge to an uneventful conclusion, with his own position intact and his reputation in the country apparently enhanced, has to count as a virtuoso political performance on Stalin's part, but what had been the point of the whole thing? Molotov, interviewed later in life, said it was necessary to eliminate a potential fifth column in the coming war. Whatever the rationales – elimination of possible fifth columns, catching foreign spies, clearing away dead wood in the administration and opening the way for promotions of the new cohort trained in the early 1930s – they seem inadequate justification for decimating the army command, the party's Central Committee and government, and the top industrial leadership. But perhaps, following the Bolsheviks' favourite French Revolutionary analogy, revolutions do have an internal logic that predisposes them to eat their own children as they themselves expire. There is also a logic that terror – as in the Revolution and then in collectivisation – begets more terror. In 1934, Stalin warned his colleagues in the leadership that destroying the 'enemy classes – capitalists, kulaks and the rest – did not get rid of the Soviet Union's security problem, since individual members of these former classes survived, not only aggrieved but now also masked and invisible to the watchful state. There undoubtedly were many such people concealing a grievance, in the party and the population in general, and the scattershot approach of the Great Purges could be seen as a means of neutralising these invisible enemies. But executing 700,000 'counter-revolutionaries' and sending a million more to Gulag was a costly way to do it.

In the aftermath of the Great Purges, the senior ranks of all institutions – party, government, military, security – were largely staffed by novices, often newly minted graduates of lower-class origins with party cards who had been rushed through training. To look at the archives of 1939 is to glimpse a devastated bureaucracy, full of missing parts and desperately trying to find people to fill the gaps, barely functional. Institutional memory had been lost; new appointees were struggling. This of course was a temporary situation: within a year or so, the jobs got filled and people learned how to do them. Possibly, overall, they did them better than their predecessors, being younger and better educated. But note the date: 1939. After all the crying wolf of earlier years, war was finally coming.

MRS MOLOTOV AND 'RED MOSCOW'

'Red Moscow' perfume, with its trademark 'onion dome' stopper

In the mid 1930s, after the hardship and stern resolve of collectivisation and the First Five Plan, the Soviet leaders decided it was time for a bit of relaxation. Food Minister Anastas Mikoyan went to the USA and came back with ice-cream and frankfurters for the Soviet consumer, with 'Soviet champagne' also added to the menu; Foreign Minister Molotov's wife, Polina Zhemchuzhina, working in the same ministry in the Edible Fats department, oversaw the marketing of a perfume, 'Red Moscow' to bring joy to the lives of socialist women. 'Red Moscow' – whose genesis in Russia before the First World War was shared with Chanel's 'No. 5' – became a great hit, and the elegant and competent Zhemchuzhina, shtetl-born and a party member since 1918, rose to become People's Commissar for Fisheries. But there were troubles ahead: in 1949, Zhemchuzhina was arrested as a Zionist (with her husband still a member of the Politburo!) and sent off into internal exile for five years, returning only after Stalin's death. She died, a Stalinist to the last, in 1970. After some fashion doldrums in the Brezhnev period, 'Red Moscow' returned to Russia in post-Soviet Russia as a nostalgia item.

Zhemchuzhina at her desk in the 1940s

4

WAR AND ITS AFTERMATH

ON 23 AUGUST 1939, Vyacheslav Molotov (newly appointed Soviet foreign minister) signed a non-aggression pact on behalf of the Soviet Union with his German counterpart, Joachim von Ribbentrop. It pledged the two countries not to attack each other, and secret protocols acknowledged their respective spheres of interest in Eastern Europe – that is, they gave each other a free hand. Bolshevism was Nazi Germany's number-one stated enemy, while fascism was the Soviet Union's. The Western world was shocked by the pact, and the international left plunged into disarray and soul-searching. The Soviet population, however, greeted it with relief: Stalin had 'bought time' before what seemed an almost inevitable war, and had perhaps even enabled the Soviet Union to stay out of the combat, letting Britain and France fight it out with Hitler. Stalin himself did not think he had bought off Hitler forever; he probably hoped for something like two years, since the Soviet Army and defence industry, still shattered by the Great Purges, were not yet ready to fight.

While the Soviet Union had moved closer to the West in the 1930s, a thick residue of distrust remained on either side. Foreign Minister Maxim Litvinov (Molotov's predecessor) had favoured alignment with the democracies, as did Soviet Ambassador Ivan Maisky in London, but Stalin and Molotov never fully went along with this. In their eyes, the Western powers, including Germany, were all 'capitalists', each as perfidious as the other. Soviet distrust of Britain and France had intensified in September 1938 with the Western powers' appeasement of Germany at Munich (a conference to which the Soviet Union was not invited), which essentially gave the green light for a German advance into Czechoslovakia's Sudetenland and, more broadly, the German pursuit of *Lebensraum* in the east.

Poland looked to be next on the Germans' list. Unlike the British, the Soviet leaders cherished no particular affection for the country or its government, but in geopolitical terms it was the buffer between Germany and the Soviet Union, and hence a major object of concern. With the secret protocols to the pact, the Soviet Union had implicitly recognised the Germans' right to take over Western Poland in return for the Soviet right to do the same in the eastern provinces it had ceded to Poland in 1921. German troops moved into Western Poland on 1 September 1939; on 3 September, Britain and France declared themselves at war with Germany, with the Soviet Union remaining neutral. Soviet troops entered eastern Poland a few weeks later.

Much has been written about the non-aggression pact as a love affair between dictators, but love was not much in evidence: if Hitler and Stalin had wanted to emphasise their personal rapprochement, they could have negotiated the pact themselves instead of sending surrogates – and, in Stalin's case, Molotov, a man whose face-to-face meeting with Hitler had left him notably unimpressed. While the intense anti-Nazi line of previous Soviet press coverage of Europe was muted, silence about the new partner, rather than a strongly positive rebranding, replaced it. The Soviet public got the message that this was not a love affair but an alliance of convenience.

The occupation of eastern Poland, quickly followed by its incorporation into the Soviet Union and the automatic granting of Soviet citizenship to its residents, was the first Soviet territorial acquisition since the end of the civil war. The Polish territories were divided between the existing Soviet republics of Ukraine and Belorussia, adding twenty-three million former Polish citizens to the population. A few months later, Soviet troops moved into the three Baltic states, former provinces of the old Russian Empire that had been independent between the wars, as well as into parts of Bessarabia, another formerly Russian imperial territory that had been under Romanian rule. The result was the addition of four more small republics to the Soviet Union – Latvia, Lithuania, Estonia and Moldavia (as the former Romanian territory was named).

This looked like a satisfactory buffer between the Soviet Union and an expansionist and belligerent Germany. As it turned out, however, it did the Soviets little good. Attempting to bully Finland into line along with the Baltics, the Soviets encountered unexpectedly firm resistance, resulting in a brief war in the winter of 1939–1940 in which the Soviet Army initially performed disastrously. It prevailed in the end, of course, given the disparity of forces, and acquired some

territory, including Karelia, but the war left Finland independent and the reputation of the Soviet Army severely damaged.
In June 1941, the Germans moved their troops right up to the
new Soviet frontier (the Soviets having not yet had time to
move their defences forward to the new borders). This move
in itself conveyed the likelihood of attack (probably in early
summer, to avoid the problem of mud and snow), but Stalin
also received explicit warning from the British, based on their
intelligence, as well as from Richard Sorge, the Soviets' spy in
Tokyo. There was no question of Stalin not knowing about the
threat of attack: according to historian Richard Overy, at least
eighty-four warnings came in, including reports of systematic
German violations of Soviet airspace. But Stalin, desperate
to avoid any 'provocation' that the Germans could use as an
excuse to attack, refused to sanction a military response. On
22 June, Operation Barbarossa began with a massive German
onslaught that destroyed the greater part of the Soviet air
force on the ground, moved Wehrmacht forces forward
across the frontier with frightening speed and had the Soviet
troops and population scrambling backward in a disorderly
retreat-cum-evacuation.

THE GREAT FATHERLAND WAR

Within days, the German Army had crossed through the newly
acquired buffer territory and reached the old Soviet frontiers;
within a week, they were in Minsk, the Belorussian capital.
Shortly thereafter, German forces moved into the Baltic states
and established German occupation regimes to replace the
recently established Soviet ones. Leningrad was encircled,

though not captured, in August. By October, the German army was in the outskirts of Moscow.

Stalin had gambled and lost – lost everything, he at first seems to have concluded. The week after the invasion, he retreated alone to his dacha outside Moscow, completely unnerved and not answering the telephone, just as he had done after an earlier political disaster, Lenin's harsh criticism of him in the 1924 'Testament'. His absence was not exactly a state secret: any listener to Radio Moscow would have deduced that something was up when Molotov, not Stalin, went on air to announce the invasion. When a delegation from the Politburo arrived at the dacha, Stalin thought they had come to arrest him, or so Politburo member Anastas Mikoyan later claimed. 'Lenin left us a great inheritance, and we fucked it up,' Stalin reportedly said to his colleagues. They didn't arrest him – nobody ever admitted having entertained such an idea – but got him out of his funk and back to Moscow. On 3 July, he went on radio to rally the nation, still with a voice not fully under control. Reverting to the Orthodox usage of his youth, he addressed his listeners as 'brothers and sisters'.

This was a sign of things to come: the war that came to be known in Soviet history as the 'Great Fatherland War' was now glossed as a war to save *Russia* from its foreign invaders rather than as a war to save the world's first socialist state. In a speech in November 1941, Stalin summoned up images of Alexander Nevsky's thirteenth-century Battle on the Ice against the Teutonic Knights, and tsarist military leader Alexander Suvorov's resistance to Napoleon. The new Russian emphasis, later balanced in internal Soviet propaganda by representation of the multi-national character of the Soviet armed forces, passed without major pushback from the non-Russian republics (although there were some muted counterclaims from Ukrainians) and probably helped to rally Russian popular support for the war effort. Certainly, morale needed strengthening in the early months: with an apparently unstoppable invasion and chaotic Soviet retreat, rumours were circulating in the western provinces that the 'Jewish Bolshevik' regime was finally about to crumble. The army was experiencing high rates of desertion and defection, and in the regions occupied by the Germans, most people seemed initially willing to accept their presence, an attitude that hardened into hostility only in the face of mistreatment by the occupiers. Others, however, had different reactions to the outbreak of the long-expected, long-feared war. Some Soviet intellectuals later remembered a feeling akin to relief: it was awful, but an easier kind of awfulness than the terror of the late 1930s, since now there was a real enemy to fight. In the armed forces, restoration of the 'frontline 100 grams' helped to maintain morale and keep up the military (and revolutionary) tradition of male bonding over vodka.

Miraculously, Moscow did not fall to the Germans in October, although government offices and many residents were evacuated eastwards. Stalin himself thought of leaving but changed his mind. Moscow's remaining citizens were serving as volunteers in 'people's defence' units, and fresh regular troops arrived in the nick of time from Siberia, but many attributed the Soviet success, above all, to 'General Winter' bogging down the German Army's supporting troops and supplies in snow.

The Germans had launched a three-prong attack, with Moscow the most northerly prong and a southern route taking them towards Baku and its oilfields. By the end of 1942, about twelve million Soviet citizens had been evacuated to the east; the government was being run largely out of Kuibyshev (now Samara) on the Volga; and 40 per cent of the Soviet Union's territory – containing 45 per cent of its population and including the whole of Ukraine, Belorussia, the Baltic states and Moldavia, much of southern Russia, Crimea and part of the Caucasus – was under German occupation. Millions of Soviet troops had been taken prisoner of war, and some millions more had been shipped to Germany as forced labourers.

The turning point came in the Volga city of Stalingrad in January 1943. After weeks of hand-to-hand fighting in the city's streets, the Soviet Army managed to defeat General Friedrich Paulus's German troops and take them, along with their commander, prisoner. That was the beginning of a long, stubbornly fought German retreat westwards, which lasted for well over a year. Since 1941, the Soviet Union had been in alliance with Britain and the United States (France having been swiftly defeated and occupied by the Germans in 1940), but no second front was opened in the west to take the pressure off the Soviet Union, despite passionate Soviet pleas and repeated Allied promises. To the east, Germany's ally, Japan, had occupied Manchuria since the early 1930s, provoking border conflicts and, in 1939, the Battle of Khalkhin Gol, in which Soviet troops were commanded by rising military star Georgy Zhukov. Soviet victory in the battle evidently convinced the Japanese that there were no easy pickings to be made here, and the two countries

German occupation of the USSR during World War II

signed a neutrality pact in April 1941. While the pact was in fact observed by both sides throughout the war, Soviet leaders continued to worry that the Japanese might break it and pull the Soviet Union into a two-front war.

For the duration of the war, the country was run by the newly created State Defence Committee, whose operational bureau consisted of Stalin, Molotov, Beria (in charge of security services) and two new candidate members of the Politburo, Mikoyan and Georgy Malenkov. By an informal division of tasks within the State Defence Committee, Stalin had prime responsibility for military matters while the rest focused on running the war economy, whose performance is generally rated as outstanding. Stalin had no direct experience of military command, but he counted himself as an expert – in the civil war he had been a leader on the Red Army's political side – and took a strong hands-on interest in the conduct of the war. Sometimes his interventions were unhelpful or even disastrous (as in his refusal to allow timely retreat in June 1941), but he nevertheless managed to work effectively with a cohort of talented generals emerging in the course of the war, notably Zhukov, the victor of Khalkhin Gol, and Konstantin Rokossovsky (newly released from prison, where he had landed as an 'enemy of the people' during the Great Purges). Stalin and Molotov were the two civilian members of the high command headed by Marshal Semyon Timoshenko. As in the civil war, Stalin, and many of his Politburo team, chose to wear military uniform for the duration, though he did not assume the title of 'generalissimus' until the war was won.

With Stalin preoccupied by the country's military efforts, his Politburo – basically the same dozen or so men who had been with him from the 1920s, plus some newer acquisitions like Khrushchev and Beria – were left to run the home front. They worked collegially and effectively, Mikoyan later remembered, the prewar atmosphere of pervasive suspicion having dissipated and Stalin willing to listen to other opinions and change his own position if convinced. In the provinces, regional party secretaries bore even greater responsibilities than before, often with a high degree of practical autonomy. At every level in the system, political leaders found themselves working closely with military leaders, forging personal as well as professional links that would continue into the postwar period.

Unusually collegial at home, on the world stage Stalin was cutting a new, charismatic figure. Previously an enigma who had never been personally encountered by other world leaders, he quickly established a good working relationship with wartime allies Winston Churchill and Franklin Roosevelt and, indeed, won their respect. In the Allied nations, the formerly demonised Soviet leader was re-imagined as a benevolent pipe-smoking 'Uncle Joe'. A similar swing in Soviet public opinion – apparently as much spontaneous as orchestrated by the regime – raised the popularity of the Allies, particularly America and Roosevelt (Churchill's advocacy of British intervention in the Russian civil war was still remembered).

Once again, war was largely a man's game. But in contrast to the civil war, women's contribution, as the mainstay of the home front, was noted, and the representation of women in the Communist Party actually rose a few points (reaching 18 per cent in 1945). Heroic women resisters under German occupation were celebrated as martyrs. Nevertheless, the grieving mother was the dominant female image associated with the war, and indeed women had something to grieve about, given the wartime carnage of their husbands and sons. Wartime losses were disproportionately men, with the result that a whole cohort of women necessarily found themselves single, albeit often single mothers. Even in 1959, the first postwar census showed close to twenty million more women than men in the population of the RSFSR, Ukraine and Belorussia.

The Soviet conduct of the war was predictably ruthless, with Stalin declaring early on – in the face of the large-scale capture of soldiers and surrender of units to the Germans – that anyone who allowed himself to be taken prisoner of war was a traitor whose family as well as himself was liable to punishment. Nevertheless, the Russian population rallied behind the war effort, perhaps to Stalin's surprise, and non-Slavic peoples outside the occupied zone, whose contribution to the war effort in support of the Russian 'older brother' was duly recognised after the first months, seem to have done likewise. (Even in the early post-Soviet Kazakhstan, with the school textbooks rewritten to support a more Kazakh-nationalist version of the country's history, the chapter on World War II remained imbued with the spirit of Soviet patriotism mobilised in the national effort to throw out the invaders.)

A Soviet propaganda poster from 1942 reads: 'Red Army Soldier, Save Us!'.

In the occupied regions, of course, it was a different story. The Germans found many collaborators in Ukraine, Belorussia and southern Russia. Mobile groups from Stepan Bandera's Organisation of Ukrainian Nationalists – directed from his base in German-occupied Poland in coordination with German military intelligence – were active in occupied Ukraine, and Cossacks, Tatars and Kalmyks departing with the Germans were prominent among the recruits to the German armed forces in the last stages of the war. When Soviet troops recaptured the Caucasus and Crimea, several small nationalities, including the Chechens and Crimean Tatars, were declared 'traitor nations' and deported, in one of Beria's typically ruthless and efficient operations, to Central Asia. One of the unanticipated consequences was that the ethnic mix in places like Kazakhstan become more diverse than ever, with defiant Chechens and hardworking ethnic Germans (deported from the Volga earlier in the war) rubbing shoulders with local Kazakhs and long-established Russian and Ukrainian settlers.

In April 1943, the Germans discovered mass graves of Polish officers in the Katyn Forest in the Smolensk region and announced it as a Soviet atrocity. So it was, although Soviet propagandists vigorously denied it and pinned the blame on the Germans, and many on the Allied side wanted to believe them. The Polish officers' capture dated back to the Soviet occupation of eastern Poland in 1939, and they appear to have been killed in the spring of 1940. Historically rocky relations with Poland were not improved when, pursuing the retreating Germans, Soviet forces arrived at the border of Poland in the summer of 1944. Anxious to make liberation from the Germans a national Polish achievement as well as a Soviet one, but also hoping for Soviet military support, the underground Polish Home Army launched an uprising in Warsaw. But the Soviet Army under General Rokossovsky sat tight on the other side of the Vistula River, citing overextended supply lines. The Soviet advance into Poland made them the first of the Allied powers to reach and liberate Nazi concentration camps, Majdanek in July 1944 and Auschwitz the following January. Famous war correspondents Ilya Ehrenburg and Vasily Grossman, both Jewish, published shocking and detailed reports on the Holocaust as they travelled westwards with the Soviet Army.

It was a race with the Allied armies to Berlin, but the Soviet Army got there first and proudly planted the Soviet flag on the Reichstag on 30 April 1945. Victory at last! And, one might

Soviet soldiers raise the Soviet flag on the Reichstag in Berlin on 2 May 1945. Photo taken by Soviet photographer Yevgeny Khaldei.

have thought, vindication for the Soviet regime. But Stalin still seemed to feel he had survived by the skin of his teeth. Given the mistakes made early on, he told an assembly of army commanders in the Kremlin in May, and the consequent German occupation of much of the country, 'Another people might have said to the government: you have not lived up to our expectations, go away, we will set up another government . . . [But] our Soviet people, above all the Russian people' did not do that. With unusual humility, Stalin's toast was 'to the Russian people for its trust'.

AFTER THE WAR

Victory Day was celebrated for the first time on 24 June 1945, in Moscow's Red Square. Marshal Zhukov, astride a white horse, was a key attraction. (Stalin had declined the role, not sure at sixty-six that his riding skills were up to it.) This was the birth of a heroic myth that was to become central to national identity – not only that of the Soviet Union but also that of the post-Soviet Russian Federation. Victory Day has been celebrated in Red Square on 9 May almost every year since 1946. As the Soviets saw it, the victory was glorious, but it was achieved at tremendous cost and essentially belonged to the Soviet Union alone, with the Allies playing supporting roles in Europe and the war in the Pacific a mere sideshow. This version of the war, of course, was different from that of the Western Allies, but there was no disagreement that the Soviet contribution had been crucial and its losses exceptionally high.

The Soviet Union had been something of a pariah on the international scene before the war, but by the end of the war it was an emergent superpower. The Big Three – Stalin, Churchill

A dashing Marshal Zhukov on a white horse at the Victory parade in Moscow, 24 June 1945

and Roosevelt – had sketched the outlines of the postwar world at their meeting at Yalta, in Crimea, in February 1945. (Even the choice of venue denoted the Soviet Union's new status: Stalin did not like flying and was unwilling to leave Soviet territory, so the ailing Roosevelt and Churchill were the ones doing the travelling.) At Yalta, the Western Allies conceded the principle of a primary Soviet interest in Eastern Europe, paving the way for the creation of a yet more substantial buffer protecting the Soviet Union from any possible aggression from Germany in the future. But it quickly became clear that given Britain's precipitous decline as an imperial power, it would not be the Big Three but the Big Two. Churchill was even voted out of office as Britain's prime minister in the middle of the Potsdam Conference. The United States and the Soviet Union were to be the postwar superpowers, no longer allies but ideological and geo-political antagonists.

The balance of might was strongly tilted to the American side, especially in the early Cold War years. The United States emerged from World War II rich, powerful, confident that its democratic principles and way of life were morally superior to communism and, for the time being, the only possessor of the atomic bomb. The Soviet Union emerged poor and economically shattered, without the bomb (but Beria and his scientists were working on it) and equally confident of its own moral superiority. It now had a buffer against aggression from the West in the form of a bloc of Soviet-dominated states in Eastern Europe. There were even early Soviet hopes (and on the American part, fears) that Western Europe – France and Italy in particular, with their popular communist parties, but also perhaps a future united

Stalin at the Potsdam Conference, July–August 1945

Germany – would follow the Soviet example and go communist. 'All of us thought it would happen because we wanted it so much,' Khrushchev later remembered. Unfortunately, the United States stepped in with the Marshall Plan – a huge economic subsidy to devastated Europe – so 'all these countries stayed capitalist, and we were disappointed'. Where revolution actually made headway in the postwar world was Asia, with Kim Il-sung establishing a Soviet-sponsored communist regime in North Korea in 1948, and Mao Zedong's Communists coming to power in China (by their own efforts, with only minimal support from Moscow) in 1949. That was welcome, as long as China understood that it was the little brother in the world communist movement; but Soviet rejoicing at this development was less notable than the almost hysterical alarm it provoked in the United States.

The Marshall Plan was not seriously offered to the Soviet Union and, under Soviet pressure, not accepted by the Soviet bloc countries of Eastern Europe. But Soviet wartime losses were tremendous and the task of reconstruction formidable. Population losses are now generally estimated at twenty-seven to twenty-eight million (though in Stalin's time the official figure given was seven million, to avoid conveying an image of weakness). Twelve million people who had evacuated to the east during the war had to return home, and the majority of the eight million in the wartime army had to be demobilised. Another five million ended the war in Germany as prisoners of war or forced labourers. With some difficulty, the Soviets succeeded in repatriating more than four million of them, but an estimated half a million remained in the capitalist world, joining the 'first-wave' emigrants of the early 1920s in an expanded

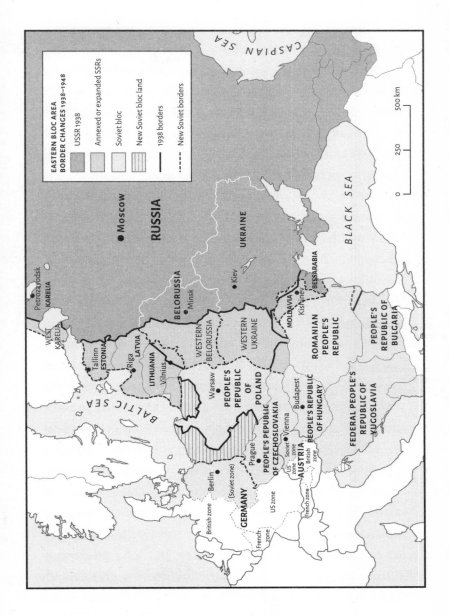

USSR and Eastern Europe, 1945

anti-Soviet emigration. The huge number of people in transit gives a sense of the magnitude of the disruption. In Leningrad, the Soviet Union's second city, the German blockade, lasting for more than three years, had killed a large proportion of the population. In the country as a whole, according to Soviet figures, almost a third of prewar capital stock had been destroyed, and in the occupied territories, where German forces had pursued a scorched-earth policy on their way out, it was two-thirds.

Eastern Europe was a cause of continual tension between the Soviets and the Western Allies, as Soviet-controlled governments that were more or less communist and more or less unpopular with local populations were clumsily installed. The Yalta agreement had always implied that a 'Soviet bloc' would be formed in Eastern Europe, but for the Western Allies – particularly the United States, with its strong ethnic lobbies – the reality was something else again. By 1947, in his famous speech in Fulton, Missouri, Churchill – now out of power, but with behind-the-scenes encouragement from both American and British leaders – pointed to an 'iron curtain' dividing a continent that, thanks to the Soviets' 'expansive and proselytising tendencies', was 'certainly not the Liberated Europe we fought to build up'. The defection in Canada of a Soviet spy, Igor Gouzenko, raised concern over spying to fever pitch, while Senator Joseph McCarthy's hunt for communist infiltrators in the US State Department and the US Army generated more alarm and disruption. In 1948, conflict over Berlin almost escalated into war, and Western concern about Soviet intentions rose sharply when the Soviet Union, playing catch-up with the Americans, successfully tested its own atomic bomb. In 1952, the Americans executed two Jewish New Yorkers, Julius and Ethel Rosenberg, for passing atomic secrets to the Soviets. In 1953, Soviet scientists, led by Igor Kurchatov under Beria's administrative direction, produced a hydrogen bomb. A third world war, bringing an unimaginable nuclear holocaust, seemed to many not only possible but likely.

All kinds of hopes had been cherished during the war that victory, if it came, would bring relaxation and general betterment. Even Mikoyan, a Politburo member close to Stalin, hoped that the 'comradely democratism' generated by wartime social relations would be carried over into civilian life. But in reality, things were never going to be easy, given the tense international situation and the huge challenges of economic reconstruction conducted without external help. Intellectuals who had hoped for an easing of censorship after the war were disappointed. Peasants who had hoped to hang on to the private plots reconstituted during the war found kolkhoz discipline re-established, and their standard of living plummeting again. Labour conscripts – villagers, urban adolescents, former forced labourers returned from Europe – and prisoners from an ever-expanding Gulag played an even larger part in the workforce than before the war. The country's economic woes were compounded by a famine in the western parts of the country in 1946–1947, less brutally handled than its 1933 precursor but a cruel blow on top of wartime devastation.

The Communist Party's membership had both changed and grown significantly, with almost two million new members added in the last prewar years, plus a similar number of new members during the war, bringing their numbers up to 5.8 million as of 1945. The 'class of '38' that came in after the Great Purges contained many young managers and professionals, better educated than their predecessors, while the wartime recruits brought with them a spirit of frontline brotherhood that became central to party culture (as it had, *mutatis mutandis*, after the civil war). The impact of the young party professionals was felt in the higher reaches of government too; as historian Julie Hessler discovered in the archives, a bunch of young 'enlightened bureaucrats' in the finance ministry were circulating proposals to legalise the urban private sector so that it could be taxed – radical reform proposals that were not acted upon but also brought no punishment to the authors. As the state budget expanded in the postwar years, so also did spending on social welfare, education and public health. The number of doctors per head of population doubled in the 1940s and added another third in the years 1950–1956, making it among the highest levels in the world at the time. For the historian Christopher Burton, this was the period when the Soviet public health system – fragmented into different levels of privilege and access during the 1930s – finally got its act together and set about universalising entitlements.

Liberalisation was to be found, rather surprisingly, in a number of spheres of postwar life. Many Orthodox churches had been allowed to reopen at the end of the war, stimulating a mini religious revival. Those lucky enough to attend Moscow State University in the late Stalin years – including Gorbachev and his wife Raisa – felt themselves part of a uniquely privileged cohort that, in the wake of wartime victory, could complete the building of socialism in the Soviet Union and iron out its prewar deficiencies; the Gorbachev cohort would always look back on their youth as a time of hope, intellectual discovery and idealism. American studies was a particularly glamorous discipline in Moscow's universities, attracting Stalin's daughter Svetlana along with a bunch of other Politburo offspring in a new generation that was about to fall in love with American writer Ernest Hemingway. Police reports of the 'popular mood', the Soviet substitute for opinion polling, routinely reported expressions of popular affection for America – 'its people, not its government' – that would persist, regardless of the Cold War, for decades.

Another kind of liberalisation could be discerned in the flourishing of bribery and corruption, with scandals even in the high courts. Confidence men found easy pickings, one (a double amputee fresh from Gulag) being so brazen in extracting money and scarce goods from ministries as a 'wounded war hero' that he got a detailed and almost admiring write-up in one of Stalin's weekly intelligence reports. Perhaps not coincidentally, the enormously popular novels of Ilya Ilf and Evgeny Petrov celebrating the exploits of a fictional conman, Ostap Bender, were temporarily banned the next year.

In the early years of the Cold War, Western journalists, anxious to discern trends of liberalisation and Westernisation, published rumours that Stalin, old and sick, would soon yield his place to an allegedly more liberal Molotov. These reports, all the more galling for being inaccurate, caused Molotov embarrassment and political demotion. But it was true that Stalin was aging. He seems to have had a heart attack in the latter half of 1945. For the sake of his health, he now spent many months of the year in the south, and even when in Moscow his daily workload – hitherto phenomenal – dropped sharply. His interventions in policy debates became more sporadic, though no less disruptive when they occurred, and his Politburo comrades were generally left to run their own shops (heavy industry, agriculture, trade and so on) with minimal interference. There were no more mass purges of the political elite, although this did not preclude localised purges such as the Leningrad Affair, which ended the career of a promising young political high-flyer, Nikolai Voznesensky. In the newly acquired regions of Western Ukraine and the Baltics, Sovietisation – which often felt like Russianisation – was conducted with a heavy hand. In Uzbekistan, on the other hand, the old indigenous party leadership had been replaced after the Great Purges by a new cohort, also indigenous but Soviet-educated, which carried on the task of mediation between Moscow and a traditionally minded Islamic population.

In a familiar dialectic, liberal and repressive tendencies coexisted in the late Stalin years. On the repressive side, Trofim Lysenko, an agricultural scientist with his own cranky agenda, managed to gain official approval for his campaign against genetics. Creativity in the arts and sciences in general was hamstrung and frustrated. It was a period of growing officially sponsored xenophobia, when schoolchildren were taught that the Russian Alexander Popov, not the Italian Guglielmo Marconi, invented the radio; contact with foreigners became dangerous; and marriages of Soviet citizens to foreigners were forbidden by law.

Most alarming of all was the growth of anti-Semitism, which appeared to have official sanction. Anti-Semitism was a familiar phenomenon in Russia, sparking pogroms in late tsarist times. But the Bolsheviks, with substantial Jewish membership and a historical aversion to anti-Semitism as a form of national discrimination, had generally steered clear of it. Stalin's Politburo contained only one Jew (Kaganovich), but more than half its members had Jewish wives or sons- and daughters-in-law. The Soviet intelligentsia formed in the 1930s had a substantial Jewish component, and there was little tolerance for anti-Semitism within it. All of this made the lurch into quasi-official anti-Semitism of the late 1940s the more aberrant and shocking to the Soviet elite, if not to the broader public. Certainly there had been warning signs of growing popular anti-Semitism during the war. The territorial acquisitions following the 1939 non-aggression pact had added two million Jews to the Soviet population, not to mention an unknowable number of anti-Semites among the newly incor- porated Western Ukrainians and Western Belorussians. After the German attack, many of these Jews fled or were deported to Siberia, Kazakhstan and Central Asia. Soon, disturbing reports were reaching Moscow of a rise in anti-Semitism in places that historically had scarcely any Jewish population. Rumours circulated that the Jews were 'sitting out the war in Tashkent' while Russians were taking the brunt of the fighting.

The official line condemning anti-Semitism never changed, but by 1947 the campaign against foreign influence, initially simply xenophobic, acquired unmistakable anti-Semitic over- tones, with 'homeless cosmopolitans' a code term for Jews. The Jewish Anti-Fascist Committee, set up during the war for inter- national propaganda and fundraising purposes, was disbanded,

JAZZ IN THE SOVIET UNION

Klavdiya Shulzhenko, the Soviet Union's Vera Lynn, performing to soldiers
at the Leningrad Front, 1941

The story is often told of the Soviet condemnation of jazz (in
the late 1930s and again in the late 1940s) as a manifestation of
Western decadence. That is one story of Soviet jazz, but there
is another – the story of its enduring popularity and repeated
resurrections with the help of highly-placed patrons. Jazz
came to the Soviet Union from Europe and America in the
1920s, and avant-garde theatre director Vsevolod Meyerhold
used it to great effect to show degenerate capitalists at play.
Its advocates, however, could argue that jazz was the music of
down-trodden American blacks. In the Soviet dance craze in
the 1930s, big bands were competitively supported, along with
sports teams, by the NKVD and other powerful institutions.
During the Second World War, jazzmen like Odessa's Leonid
Utesov (a personal favourite of Stalin's) performed at the

front, and Klavdiya Shulzhenko – the Soviet Union's Vera Lynn – immortalised front-line comradeship in the jazzy 'Let's have a smoke'. Some added balalaikas and accordions as folk colouration, but not Polish jazz trumpeter Eddie Rosner, a 1939 Jewish refugee from the Nazis, who founded the State Jazz Orchestra of Belorussia with republican party patronage and became another wartime star. After the war, the anti-cosmopolitan campaign sent Rosner to Gulag (where a sympathetic camp director let him form a jazz band) and kept Oleg Lundstrem, a postwar Russian repatriate from the Shanghai jazz scene, confined to Kazan, albeit under the protection of jazz-loving patrons in the local party leadership. But by 1956, Rosner and Lundstrem were both leading jazz ensembles in Moscow.

Eddie Rosner was released and rehabilitated after Stalin's death, leading a big band and still playing the trumpet, despite having lost his teeth due to malnutrition in the camps.

and its leading members were arrested, along with high-ranking political patron Solomon Lozovsky, and in the summer of 1952 convicted of treason in a closed military court and shot. The announcement in December 1952 of the unmasking of a 'doctors' plot' in the Kremlin Hospital to kill Politburo members and spy for foreign intelligence was the alarming culmination. While the doctors were not formally identified in newspaper reports as Jewish, their full names and patronymics were given, making their ethnicity clear to all Soviet readers. Popular denouncers took up the anti-Semitic theme, stressing Jewish privilege and corruption, while at the same time rumours flew around that the government was planning to deport all Jews to the hinterland, as had been the fate of 'traitor' nationalities such as Chechens and Crimean Tatars during the war.

This semi-covert anti-Semitic campaign appears to have been a personal initiative of Stalin's, disconcerting almost all of his Politburo. It coincided with a determined effort by Stalin to undermine some of his closest Politburo colleagues, notably Molotov, Voroshilov and Mikoyan, by suggesting that they were hand in glove with the Americans and the Jews. Of course, Molotov and Mikoyan *had* had extensive contact with Americans, given their respective positions as ministers of foreign affairs and foreign trade. This was considered relevant to the Jewish issue because the new Jewish state of Israel, whose creation Stalin had supported, was now a de facto ally of the United States. Molotov's Jewish wife was arrested in 1949 for Zionist sympathies and sent into exile, but it was not only Molotov whose neck was on the block. The malign imagination that had woven links between virtually all former

Oppositionists, whether of left or right, and Trotsky and his presumed foreign intelligence backers in 1936–1938 would surely have no trouble implicating Beria (a consistent supporter of Israel in the Politburo), Kaganovich (a Jew), Malenkov (whose daughter had married Lozovsky's son) and who knows who else in the new Moscow show trial scenario that Stalin seemed to be building. This explains the otherwise extraordinary fact that when Stalin tried to freeze Molotov and Mikoyan out of the Politburo's social network in the last months of 1952, none of the rest of the Politburo backed him up.

International tensions had been growing steadily between the two superpowers. Both now had the bomb, and the size of the Soviet Army had risen from under three million in 1948 to over five million by 1953. In mid-1950, North Korea, the Soviet Union's client, invaded the US client South Korea, admittedly against Stalin's strong advice. In the three-year-long Korean War that followed, the Soviet Union was officially non-belligerent, but both the United States and China were militarily involved on opposing sides. US fears of the spread of world communism led to pressure in the Republican Party to repudiate the Yalta agreement and free the 'captive nations' in the communist bloc. According to Khrushchev's later memoirs, 'In the days leading up to Stalin's death, we believed that America would invade the Soviet Union and we would go to war.' Stalin, personally, was terrified, desperately trying (shades of 1941) to avoid giving any pretext for attack. Presumably this was a response to the liberationist rhetoric of John Foster Dulles, who became secretary of state after Republican Dwight Eisenhower's election to the US presidency in November 1952. If in retrospect it looks like an overreaction, that does not detract from the reality of the fear. In the Kremlin, it seems to have been one of those moments when inchoate threats loom from every direction and every nightrider might be one of the horsemen of the apocalypse.

The end was indeed nigh, but it was not the Last Judgement or even a capitalist invasion. We shall never know how the Soviet political manoeuvring of the winter of 1952–1953 might have played out, because it was cut off abruptly by an act of God: on 5 March 1953, Stalin died. The circumstances of his death, following a stroke when he was alone at his dacha, have been immortalised in Armando Iannucci's 2017 film *The Death of Stalin*, which for all its insouciance about details, captures the essential black comedy of the situation. Politburo members, hastily summoned when Stalin was found unconscious, were slow to call a doctor – but who was there to call, given that most of the Kremlin doctors, including Stalin's own, were in prison? Relieved though some Politburo members may have been at the prospect of Stalin's death, there is no evidence of individual or group complicity. They shared an awkward vigil at his bedside, with Beria more or less assuming command. But even before Stalin had breathed his last, the Politburo – including its formerly ostracised members, Molotov and Mikoyan – was meeting in Stalin's Kremlin office to decide the composition of the new government and write the press release. This was business as usual to an almost bizarre degree; apocalyptic premonitions had evidently died with Stalin. The Soviet Union had a new 'collective leadership' – in effect, Stalin's Politburo, minus Stalin. What that contradiction in terms meant remained to be seen.

5

FROM 'COLLECTIVE LEADERSHIP' TO KHRUSHCHEV

EVERY SOVIET CITIZEN WOULD ALWAYS remember where they were when they heard the news of Stalin's death, like Americans on the day of President Kennedy's assassination. Some no doubt privately rejoiced, but the immediate reaction of many was grief, combined with fear for the future – how will we manage without Stalin to look after us? The funeral was marred by a stampede of people pouring onto the Moscow streets, hoping for a last sighting of the leader or just curious. Typical of the serendipitous quality of Soviet history, it was not a crowd of protesters or even worshippers; it was more like a crowd in search of a meaning. But people were trampled to death in the crush, and the whole episode left a feeling of foreboding.

The familiar short version of Soviet history has the exit of Stalin the tyrant followed immediately by the entrance of Khrushchev the reformer. But things were odder than that. It was Stalin's old Politburo – in which Khrushchev ranked about number five – that collectively stepped forward with an immediate program of radical reform so coherent and comprehensive that you would think they had worked it out in advance. None of them ever admitted to this, and given the degree of surveillance they were under in Stalin's last years, it would have been incredibly risky. But there is no avoiding the conclusion that a consensus on the need for wide-reaching change 'when the time comes' had quietly developed among Stalin's associates.

The general opinion on Stalin's closest political colleagues, held by both their contemporaries and historians, is that they were a bunch of spineless hacks, yes-men for their leader and totally under his thrall. The mean age of these men – Molotov, Mikoyan, Khrushchev, Beria, Voroshilov, Kaganovich, Malenkov – was around sixty, with Voroshilov (born 1881) and Malenkov (born 1901) at the two extremes. They had gone through the Purges with Stalin, both as co-executants and potential victims; worked collegially with him and each other during the war; and endured the uneasy postwar years, with Stalin often absent, increasingly erratic and, towards the end, probably out for their blood. Loyalty to Stalin, one might have thought, was in their DNA, but while none of them ever wholly repudiated him, clearly most had private doubts and reservations. A telling anecdote comes from Stepan Mikoyan, adult son of Politburo member Anastas Mikoyan, who sought to impress his father by telling him that he had paid his last respects as Stalin's body lay in state before the funeral. 'You were wasting your time,' his father said curtly. Stepan, brought up to venerate Stalin, was shocked: 'It was the first signal that there could be a critical attitude to Stalin, and that my father had that attitude.'

In the new government, Malenkov held the top state job as chairman of the Council of Ministers; Beria, in his old job as head of security, seemed the most dynamic figure; and Molotov, back heading foreign affairs, was the elder statesman. Mikoyan was in charge of trade, Bulganin of defence (with Marshals Aleksandr Vasilevsky and Georgy Zhukov of World War II–fame as deputies) and Khrushchev was secretary (not 'general secretary' like Stalin) of the party.

Two days after Stalin's funeral, Beria released Molotov's wife from exile and had her flown in from Kazakhstan for reunion with her husband. Radical policy reforms were quickly introduced and followed each other in dizzying succession. On Beria's initiative, prosecutions in the 'doctors' plot' were stopped, the doctors released and their freedom announced in the press. Next on the list, also a Beria initiative, was a mass amnesty in Gulag, starting with a million 'non-political' prisoners, but soon moving on, albeit more gradually, to the politicals. In the Baltic republics, the Russianising direction was reversed, with Beria insisting on promoting locals at a cracking pace (when the Latvian branch of the secret police told him they had run out of Latvian candidates who were not blacklisted as nationalists, Beria said that was irrelevant). Stalin's name, hitherto ubiquitous, suddenly disappeared from the newspapers; publication of his collected works was abruptly halted. Agricultural reforms were introduced to raise the dismally low living standards in the countryside. Retail prices were cut sharply, and Malenkov took on the task of making more consumer goods available to the urban population. Reform-minded editors were appointed to the major 'thick' literary journals, which even under Stalin had functioned as a kind of civil-society enclave.

When the team, announcing itself as a 'collective leadership', appeared in public together, observers noted the easy comradeship of their interactions, very different from the stiff formality of late Stalinist appearances. The Soviet Union's new leaders were 'blossoming like leathery cacti', commented American correspondent Harrison Salisbury. The US administration was slower to respond to the change, though the new Soviet leaders were doing all they could to signal it. Malenkov's eulogy at Stalin's funeral was a passionate plea for peace and international cooperation that made only perfunctory mention of the deceased. A few months after Stalin's death, the Soviet Union agreed to a truce in the Korean War. President Eisenhower noticed these feelers and wondered if they should be taken seriously, but he was persuaded otherwise by Dulles, who knew that the cunning Soviet leopard could never really change his spots. Experts from the new discipline of Sovietology, going under the banner of 'Know your enemy', confirmed that totalitarian societies like the Soviet Union and Nazi Germany were incapable of reform and would collapse only when defeated in war. US unresponsiveness lent credibility to the view of hardliners such as Molotov in the collective leadership that there was really no point in making overtures to the West: the imperialist leopard could never change his spots . . .

In June 1953, the collective leadership cast out and subsequently executed one of its own – the most energetic and radical of the reformers, head of the secret police Lavrenty Beria. They were afraid he had too much dirt on them personally, that he was using *kompromat* (compromising material out of police files) on republican and regional leaders to build a national support network, that he was encouraging his own personality cult in his native Georgia and that he didn't really care about socialism. They also thought he was a show-off who lacked real respect for his colleagues. (Kaganovich for one was fed up with hearing from Beria that 'I am the authority, I am the liberal, after Stalin I give the amnesties, I make the exposés, I do everything'.) Beria's arrest, which took the victim totally aback, was orchestrated by Khrushchev and marked the latter's first step towards the front of the post-Stalin leadership. The anti-Beria action was accompanied by a huge smear campaign, which particularly (though untypically for the Soviet Union) focused on his sex life. A closed military court convicted him of treason and imposed the death sentence in December 1953.

It was a truth universally acknowledged in the West that a Soviet Politburo in possession of power must be in want of a leader. Thus by definition, the years 1953–1957 – the period of 'collective leadership' – was a mere *interregnum* during which the future leader emerged and got rid of his rivals, just like 1923–1927 had been. The Soviet public probably thought like that too, and the political elite as well, but only up to a point. There was certainly a Soviet tradition of having a vozhd' at the top, but there was also a tradition of collective leadership – meaning a small group of party leaders (usually called 'the Politburo', though from 1952 to 1966 it was 'the Presidium') whose members had curatorial responsibility for various sectors such as defence, trade and heavy industry, met frequently as a collective with the vozhd' in the chair and did a lot of the heavy lifting of government. This had been the model under Lenin and, *mutatis mutandis*, under Stalin. For the new leaders, both a Politburo and a vozhd' were the norm, and it was within the norm to have a Politburo without a vozhd' but not vice versa. It appears that, in the wake of Stalin's death, some members of the new leadership – including Malenkov, Mikoyan and Molotov, the last initially the putative frontrunner for any vozhd' position – genuinely wanted a collective leadership without a new vozhd', while others, notably Beria and Khrushchev, privately hoped to win the position of vozhd' for themselves.

The collective leadership were reformers who had never announced themselves as such but simply started reforming. This was in part to avoid the tricky question of their relationship to their old boss, Stalin, and the bloodshed that had occurred under his rule. Getting rid of Beria helped, since as security chief he could be portrayed as Stalin's evil genius and blamed for terror. Still, it was hard to blame him for the excesses of collectivisation, which as a republican secretary in Georgia he had quite successfully mitigated, or for the Great Purges, since he was brought to Moscow to head the secret police only as they were ending, to do the mopping up.

The Great Purges were almost twenty years in the past, yet the question of how to deal with them was growing more and more prickly. Victims were returning from Gulag, contacting old friends (including members of the collective leadership) and telling hair-raising stories. They wanted their reputations back, not to mention their Moscow residence permits and apartments; reform-minded journals wanted to publish their memoirs. 'Out of sight, out of mind' was increasingly untenable as a strategy. A commission under Central Committee secretary Peter Pospelov, known as a diehard Stalinist, was appointed in December 1955 to investigate exactly what had happened in the Great Purges. It came up with a shocking seventy-page report stating that between 1935 and 1940, almost two million people had been arrested for 'anti-Soviet activity' and 688,503 had been shot. The Politburo debated what to do about these findings (which, of course, were bound to be leaked). Mikoyan, never particularly bloodthirsty and chairman of the commission on the rehabilitation of former political prisoners since 1954, was in favour of coming clean; Voroshilov, Kaganovich and Molotov, who had the most to lose, were less enthusiastic. In the end, Khrushchev seized the initiative, delivering an unscheduled report at the Twentieth Party Congress on 25 February 1956.

The most startling part of Khrushchev's speech dealt with the impact of Stalinist terror on the upper echelons of the party. The delegates gasped when he said that 70 per cent of Central Committee members (98 out of 139) had been victims of the Great Purges. They gasped again when, turning to more recent times, he said that 'had Stalin remained at the helm for another several months, Comrades Molotov and Mikoyan would probably have not delivered any speeches at this congress'. Khrushchev criticised the 'excesses' of collectivisation (though not collectivisation itself), the destruction of the military high command in 1937, Stalin's 'mistakes' during the war (particularly episodes involving Ukraine, where Khrushchev, as republican party secretary, had clashed with him), the wartime deportation of small nationalities like the Chechens and

Crimean Tatars, the Leningrad Affair and the anti-Semitic campaign of Stalin's last years. He even hinted that Stalin might have been behind Sergei Kirov's assassination.

Khrushchev's speech was labelled 'the Secret Speech' in the West, and indeed a vain attempt was made to keep it from the West (foiled by Polish delegates to the congress, who leaked it, and the CIA, which gave it worldwide distribution). But domestically it was no secret at all, for it was read out in its entirety at party meetings held throughout the country (and open to those who were not party members). A passionate public discussion followed, with many different viewpoints expressed. Veterans were upset at the criticism of Stalin's wartime leadership. Students and intellectuals were excited at the implied prospect of cultural liberalisation. In some Russian provincial towns, it stimulated attacks on corruption in local party leaderships; in Central Asia, the issue was Russian 'colonial' attitudes in the republics' administration. The only actual civil unrest within the Soviet occurred in Tbilisi, Georgia, where after days of largely peaceful demonstrations marking the third anniversary of Stalin's death, a military unit opened fire, killing twenty-one people.

It was another story in Eastern Europe, where the Secret Speech sparked a crisis in Poland and Hungary. Poland's veteran communist leader Boleslaw Bierut, in hospital in Moscow, read it and died of heart attack. The situation in Poland – with Władysław Gomulka, recently released from prison, poised to take over the Polish party leadership without Moscow's approval, and agitation for the removal of Polish-born Soviet citizen Marshal Konstantin Rokossovsky as defence minister – looked so alarming that almost the entire Soviet Politburo, plus Marshals Zhukov and Warsaw Pact commander Ivan Konev, flew to Warsaw. That fire was put out, at the price of accepting Gomulka and sacrificing Rokossovsky, but within a week Hungary went into freefall, cheered on by the West, and in October, after agonising deliberations and many changes of mind, Soviet troops were sent into Budapest. This ultimately stabilised the situation and prevented what the Soviet Union most feared, the defection of an Eastern European country from the Soviet bloc Warsaw Pact, but at great reputational cost. With governments and the general public in the West outraged by the crushing of the Hungarian Revolution, China was one of the Soviet Union's few supporters in this action – but Mao was unhappy for another reason, namely Khrushchev's condemnation of Stalin, which to the Chinese Communists smacked of the dreaded 'revisionism' (loss of revolutionary fervour and softness on capitalism).

Khrushchev, though formally still only one among equals in the Politburo, was clearly flexing his muscles, pushing Malenkov (head of the Soviet government) off centre stage and starting to challenge Molotov. It was Khrushchev and his sidekick, Nikolai Bulganin, who set off to make friends in Europe in 1955, swanning around in matching baggy purplish summer suits that were the wonder of the West. While the development of good relations with the West was set back by the events in Hungary, building up the Soviet image in the Third World was on the agenda: Khrushchev and Bulganin went to India in 1955, and on a follow-up visit, Marshal Zhukov was photographed riding an elephant.

The Western view of Khrushchev as a lower-class comic turn was to a fair degree shared in the Soviet Union. This was particularly true of the intelligentsia, but a broader Soviet public also preferred more gravitas in a leader. Leadership contests in a Soviet context were not decided by popular vote, however, and Khrushchev's annihilation of Beria had shown what a wily political operator lay beneath that Ukrainian peasant shirt. In 1957, when a majority of Khrushchev's Politburo colleagues tried to rein him in, he turned the tables on them and emerged the victor, adding insult to injury by labelling his opponents – including Kaganovich and Molotov, for whom the party was their whole life – the 'Anti-Party Group'. Their defeat was engineered at an extraordinary meeting of the party's Central Committee, the organ that formally elected the Politburo. As in Stalin's time, many of the Central Committee's members were regional party secretaries, and, like Stalin, Khrushchev oversaw party appointments in his capacity as head of the secretariat in Moscow. In case anything went wrong, Khrushchev had Marshal Zhukov onside, but as all went well, no army intervention was needed.

Khrushchev was proud of having presided over the first Soviet leadership change that was not followed by major reprisals against the defeated. It was indeed a happy precedent, as Khrushchev no doubt had cause to reflect when his time came seven years later. All the old guard except Mikoyan were voted off the Politburo and sent to lesser jobs far from Moscow – Kaganovich to head a potash plant in the Urals, Malenkov to direct a hydro-electric station in Kazakhstan and Molotov to be Soviet Ambassador to Outer Mongolia. (Annoyingly, both Malenkov and Molotov, displaying exemplary party discipline and work ethic, did so well at their new jobs that they had to be moved to lesser positions.)

THE KHRUSHCHEV ERA

If Khrushchev was not the originator of post-Stalin reforms, as is often claimed, he was still an energetic innovator – and sometimes, according to his detractors, a 'harebrained schemer' – who led the Soviet Union in its years of greatest economic success. GNP grew at a rate of almost 7 per cent a year throughout the 1950s, compared with less than 3 per cent in the United States (the Soviet GNP admittedly starting from a lower base); industrial production in 1960 was almost three times what it had been in 1950 and close to five times the 1940 level; and agricultural production was also up. More than half the Soviet population was urban by 1962; adult literacy, not much above 50 per cent in the mid-1920s, was now close to 100 per cent. New consumer goods started to reach the urban and even the rural population: by 1965, 32 per cent of households had TV sets, 17 per cent had refrigerators and 29 per cent had washing machines. Life expectancy, which had been below forty in the middle of the 1920s, was in the high sixties twenty years later – within sight of catching up with the United States, which in the 1920s had been far ahead. For the only time in Soviet history, the claim (loudly made by Khrushchev) that the Soviet Union would soon catch up with and surpass the West actually looked plausible.

As a reformer, Khrushchev's forte was thinking big. His own formative administrative experience had been in the heyday of Stalin's first Five-Year Plan and cultural revolution of the early 1930s, and that was a spirit he tried to recapture. His ambitious Virgin Lands program was designed to bring large areas of Kazakhstan into use for growing grain, not only through large state investment but also through mobilising the enthusiasm and adventurous spirit of the young. *That* was how you built socialism, in Khrushchev's view. He never forgot the 'joy and excitement' of a campaign that, as he wrote a little sadly in his post-retirement memoirs, 'showed us how mighty our party could be if it only had the trust of the people'. Comrades' courts at local level and volunteer *druzhinniki* (something like a Soviet version of Neighbourhood Watch) were other examples of the grassroots participation encouraged in the Khrushchev years. Party membership grew from just under seven million in 1954 to eleven million in 1964 – still preponderantly men, but with women inching up to 21 per cent of membership.

Druzhinniki could, of course, turn out to be bullies of non-conformists, and Khrushchev's version of participatory socialism included campaigns against 'social parasites' – people who didn't work but made a living on the fringes of the grey economy. True to the spirit of the cultural revolution of his youth, Khrushchev also reversed the postwar trend towards greater tolerance of religion, closing churches, harassing clergy and introducing mandatory courses in 'Scientific atheism' in universities. At village level, propagandists pointed out that cosmonauts had now flown into space but had seen no sign of God. The empty space where the Cathedral of Christ the Saviour had once stood in Moscow (intended in the 1930s for a Palace of Soviets that was never built) was turned into a remarkable year-round outdoor swimming pool, where winter swimmers were protected from the icy air outside by a cushion of steam.

For Khrushchev, the Soviet Union was a product of workers' revolution, and he never lost his identification with workers and peasants. The affirmative action policies that had taken him to the Industrial Academy in 1930 had long vanished from the Soviet Union proper (although Eastern Europe, as well as the territories incorporated into the Soviet Union in 1939, got a taste of them after the war), but they still seemed good to Khrushchev, and to the annoyance of the education profession and the intelligentsia, he revived them, though with only partial success.

Primary education had already become close to universal in the 1930s; in the 1950s and '60s it was secondary education that was expanding by leaps and bounds. Between 1939 and 1959, the percentage of the population aged ten and over possessing some post-primary education more than tripled, and the increase continued in the next intercensal period, with the percentage of twenty- to twenty-nine-year-old high-school graduates doubling between 1959 and 1970 to reach 53 per cent.

The Soviet Union had always aspired to be a welfare state (although it never used the term), but in the Khrushchev period this started to be a reality. When British economist Alec Nove asked in 1960, 'Is the Soviet Union a welfare state?', it was a new question in Sovietology. Nove's answer was yes, citing old-age and disability pensions (raised and universalised by a reform of 1956), sickness and maternity benefits, paid holidays and a reduction of the work week (including a move towards reintroducing the non-working 'weekend', abolished by the revolution). The number receiving old age and disability pensions rose from one to fourteen million between 1959 and 1970.

It was in urban housing that Khrushchev launched his most ambitious social-welfare project. Since the 1920s, virtually no new residential housing had been built, and the urban population was squashed into crowded communal apartments or, in the case of students and single workers newly arrived from the village, dormitories and barracks. Khrushchev launched a massive building program, using prefabricated materials, that enabled more than 100 million people to move into new apartments between 1956 and 1965. Of course, there were problems with the ubiquitous five-storey blocks – nicknamed *khrushchoby*, a play on the Russian word for slums (*trushchoby*) – that sprang up in new 'micro-districts' that were meant to be served by newly built shops and transport systems, but initially weren't. But it meant that a hundred million families now had their own kitchen table and even, with luck, separate bedrooms for parents and children.

Sitting round the kitchen table – in other words, socialising with family and friends in a private space – might stand as an emblem of the Khrushchev period, for it made possible the emergence of what in the West was called civil society, something separate from the state in which a public opinion could grow. Also contributing to this growth were new, albeit limited, possibilities of travel abroad, as the firmly closed borders that under Stalin had held Western culture as well as spies at bay were relaxed. In 1939, the Soviet Union had had just under five million white-collar workers with higher education (3 per cent of the workforce), but by 1959 it was eight million, and by 1970 it was fifteen million (6 per cent of the workforce) and growing. To Western eyes, this looked like a middle class, but that had bad connotations ('bourgeoisie') in the Soviet Union. So the term 'intelligentsia' was used – and perhaps something of its pre-revolutionary predecessor's idealism and high sense of moral mission did survive within the group, despite the fact that by now most of its members were Soviet-educated children of working-class and peasant parents.

In culture, the Khrushchev period is remembered as the Thaw (after the eponymous novel by Ilya Ehrenburg), suggestive of the melting of ice and snow after a hard winter. As anybody who has been in Russia during an actual thaw will know, it generates a lot of mud, and all sorts of rubbish hidden under

New housing in Moscow, 1963

the snow through winter suddenly appears, stinking, and has to be dealt with. Khrushchev's Secret Speech was a part of that process. But the Thaw also has another aspect, namely the almost visceral excitement associated with the first hints of spring after the hard Russian winter. There was a heady sense that anything was possible – even communism, whose arrival within twenty years Khrushchev rashly predicted in 1961.

For the intelligentsia, it seemed not only that it had become possible to write things that had formerly been forbidden but that it was a civic duty. Vladimir Dudintsev's novel *Not by Bread Alone* lambasted 'bureaucrats' who were the enemies of creativity. Aleksandr Solzhenitsyn's autobiographically based Gulag novella, *One Day in the Life of Ivan Denisovich*, was approved by Khrushchev for publication in the thick journal *Novy Mir* after one of those epic battles with the censor that marked the era. When something 'daring' appeared in one of the journals, everyone rushed to buy a copy; when the censors blocked publication, the grapevine spread the news all over Moscow and Leningrad. There was formal experimentation in the arts too (an exhibition of Picasso's work caused a sensation in Moscow), but the 'truth-telling' impulse predominated. Evgeny Evtushenko read his poems in sports stadiums to audiences of thousands. Premieres of Dmitry Shostakovich's new works, widely understood as protests against state repression of the lonely artist, brought concert audiences to tears. Historians rediscovered a 'democratic Lenin' as an example for the present, lawyers a Lenin with a respect for legality, and economists a Lenin whose introduction of NEP had allowed a partial revival of a market economy.

Khrushchev scored an enormous international and domestic success when the Soviet space program launched Sputnik in 1957 and then, in 1961, made Yuri Gagarin the first man in space. This rattled the United States, which, as with atomic and hydrogen weapons technology a few years earlier, had assumed it had a natural monopoly on space exploration. Khrushchev was greatly excited by his first visit to the United States in 1959: everything that he saw fascinated him, from skyscrapers and freeways to capitalists ('right out of the posters painted during our civil war – only they didn't have the pigs' snouts our artists always gave them'). The West was fascinated by him too, although reactions were mixed. When he took off a shoe and banged it on the podium at the United Nations in response to a suggestion that the Soviet Union acted as an imperialist in Eastern Europe, this was seen as crude at home as well as abroad. His famous taunt that 'History is on our side. We will bury you' was read as a threat rather than what it actually was, an angry restatement of a Marxist truism (socialism historically succeeds capitalism).

But there were a lot of things not going the Soviet way in international relations. China, the only other great power to have installed a communist regime, through revolution in 1949, threw off the Soviet Union's 'big brother' tutelage, expelled its Soviet advisers and split the world communist movement in 1961. Germany remained a chronic Cold War problem, with the German Democratic Republic part of the Soviet bloc and the Federal Republic of Germany an American client. West Berlin, almost a parody of the bright lights and fleshpots of capitalism, proved so alluring that, embarrassingly, the Berlin

Wall had to be built to keep East Germans down on the farm, or at least to keep them producing 'German quality work' in factories that were the best in the Soviet bloc.

Khrushchev may sometimes have been perceived by the West as a sabre-rattler, but he actually kept a fairly tight rein on military spending. In a private conversation with Eisenhower, the two of them agreed that 'leaders of the armed forces can be very persistent in claiming their share when it comes time to allocate funds', and Khrushchev was by no means a soft touch for military lobbyists. He cut the army down to under two and a half million (justifying this with the argument that in the modern world it was missiles that counted, not ground troops) and reduced both total spending and officers' pay. He even sidelined his former friend Marshal Zhukov, allegedly on

Khrushchev bangs his shoe at the UN General Assembly, 1960.

suspicion of Bonapartist ambitions – a particularly ungrateful, though prudent, act, given that it was Khrushchev himself who had brought Zhukov into politics by seeking his support in the actions against Beria and the 'Anti-Party Group'.

IN THE REPUBLICS

The party program of October 1961 included a new ideological formulation on the national question: the drawing together (*sblizhenie*) of Soviet nationalities would ultimately produce fusion (*sliianie*), resulting in a single Soviet identity. But that was a reminder of a long-term goal, not a signal that force was about to be applied. On the ground, the effect of Khrushchev's Thaw was to stimulate a renaissance of national cultures, freed from the rigid confines of Stalinist controls, but not anti-Soviet, and generously funded by the Soviet state. Soviet affirmative action programs of the 1930s were bearing fruit in the form of new indigenous elites, Soviet-trained but with their particular ethnic colourations. Increasingly, these elites were essentially running their republics, sometimes with one of their own in the top job of republican first secretary. But how this looked on the ground varied a great deal, depending on which republic you were looking at.

Ukraine did well under Khrushchev. From his period of service there, he had plenty of Ukrainian political friends whom he not only supported in their leadership of the republic but also brought to Moscow into top positions. If Stalin's suspicions of Ukrainians had resulted in their under-representation on the Central Committee in Moscow, their numbers rose rapidly under Khrushchev (from sixteen in 1952 to fifty-nine in 1961, producing a slight over-representation in terms of total population share). Historically an industrial powerhouse, Ukraine was back in the game, with increased republican control, after a rapid postwar reconstruction of its industry. In 1954, fulfilling an ambition he had formed back in 1944 when he was the Ukrainian party leader, Khrushchev organised the administrative transfer of Crimea from Russia to Ukraine (storing up trouble for the post-Soviet future).

The Central Asian republics, created somewhat artificially in the early 1920s, were starting to develop a sense of national particularity. This coexisted with the shared identity dictated by geography and an 'Islamic way of life' – embracing marriage and death rituals, male circumcision, festivals and the patriarchal family – which had largely survived the challenges of the 1920s and '30s. Khrushchev visited the region and liked to show it off as an example of Soviet development policy to the Third World. In terms of the flow of resources between Moscow and Central Asia, the latter was the winner. Dams and infrastructure were built, with the different republics all competitively lobbying Moscow for their share and thus reinforcing a sense of national distinction relative to the others. Uzbek leader Nuritdin Mukhitdinov, one of Khrushchev's regional supporters in his confrontation with the Anti-Party Group, was the first Central Asian elected to the Politburo.

Latvia had chafed under the reimposition of Soviet rule in 1945, and although its leader in the 1940s and '50s was a Latvian – Old Bolshevik Jānis Kalnbērziņš, who had spent part of the interwar period in Moscow – the local Communist Party, like others in the Baltic, struggled for credibility in the face of popular resentment of 'Russian' rule. The Latvian party leadership was one of two republican elites accused of nationalism in 1959 – and indeed it *was* leaning towards policies discriminating against Russians in an effort to increase its legitimacy with the Latvian population. The other republican government in trouble in 1959 was that of Azerbaijan, where a defiant leadership had, contrary to federal law, mandated study of Azeri language in all schools in the republic, including those serving sizeable national minorities (Russian, Armenian, Georgian). They were also found guilty of economic nationalism, namely in opposing construction of the Kara-Dag gas pipeline to Tbilisi, with the chair of the Azerbaijani Council of Ministers stating, 'This gas is ours, and we cannot give it to the Georgians.'

In contrast to Ukraine, the Caucasus in general was suffering from a loss of status in the Union following Stalin's death and Beria's disgrace: while Georgians and Armenians were over-represented in the Soviet Central Committee in the last years of Stalin's life, their representation had been halved by 1961. In their own republics, however, they ran things their way. Georgia, with Georgian Vasily Mzhavanadze entrenched as first secretary for almost two decades, became renowned both for nationalist oppression of local minorities such as the Abkhazians and South Ossetians, and for corruption. Such a high degree of private enterprise was tolerated as to make tourists wonder if they had inadvertently left the Soviet Union.

Khrushchev was generally in favour of giving more freedom of action to regional leaderships. From his own days as a republican party secretary, he remembered the annoyance of endless instructions from Moscow ministerial bureaucrats who didn't understand conditions on the ground, and he thought regional party secretaries should be given scope to follow their own judgement. In 1957, he pushed through a plan to dissolve the central industrial ministries and create regional economic councils (*sovnarkhozy*) in their place – a move that had the side benefit of weakening the central government bureaucrats (who were not part of his power base) and strengthening the regional party secretaries (who were). This reform trod on multiple bureaucratic toes and encountered major implementation problems, but in 1962 Khrushchev tried to push further, with a bifurcation of republican and regional party committees to deal respectively with agriculture and industry, each branch having its first secretary. This meant treading on the toes of his own power base. A third of the regional party committees never actually split, and the whole program, considered one of Khrushchev's 'harebrained schemes', was dropped immediately after his fall.

KHRUSHCHEV'S FALL

Mikoyan, though generally a Khrushchev ally, thought that Khrushchev 'got conceited' after his victory over the Anti-Party Group and started to feel that 'he didn't have to reckon with anyone'. But there was, in fact, a Politburo to reckon with, not to mention something like a public opinion. Politburo colleagues winced when in various meetings with the intelligentsia, intended as an overture to 'civil society', Khrushchev lost his cool, denouncing modern art as 'dog-shit', calling sculptor Ernst Neizvestny 'a faggot' and getting into a shouting match with Evtushenko. After one well-fuelled rant at a social

Khrushchev at the art exhibition at Moscow Manège, 1962

gathering with intelligentsia luminaries, when Khrushchev broke the rules by referring to internal Politburo disagreement in the presence of non-Communists, Kaganovich commented acidly that 'What the sober man has on his mind is on the drunk's lips'.

Two events placed the nails in his political coffin. The first was a workers' strike in Novocherkassk in southern Russia in the summer of 1962, brought on by a raising of production quotas that coincided with much-resented price hikes for meat and butter. In another country, at another time, this might seem rather ho-hum news, but the Soviet Union didn't do strikes and riots (Tbilisi in 1956 was a rare exception), so it was a shock, and the regional leadership coped with it badly. Troops opened fire on demonstrators outside the Novocherkassk party committee building, resulting in at least twenty-four fatalities.

GAGARIN IN SPACE

Soviet pilot and cosmonaut Yuri Gagarin became the first man to voyage into space, orbiting the earth in the Vostok 1 capsule in April 1961. The flight made him a national hero and caused great

chagrin to the Americans, who had considered themselves frontrunners in what became known as the Cold War 'space race'. US embarrassment was compounded a week later by the conspicuous failure of the CIA-sponsored invasion of Cuba at the Bay of Pigs.

In the wake of the flight, the young, smiling and photogenic Gagarin became an international celebrity, touring the world from Europe to the Americas (but not the United States, which banned him from visiting). His popularity was even greater in the Soviet Union. Russians were particularly proud of this native son, who combined humble origins (he was born on a collective farm in the Smolensk region in 1934) with a historically-resonant aristocratic surname. Gagarin's ethnicity was celebrated, tongue in cheek, in an anonymous ditty that became Russian urban folklore:

> How good it is that our Gagarin
> Is not a Ukrainian bumpkin or a Tatar
> Not a Kirghiz or an Uzbek
> But one of us, a real Soviet man.[1]

---

1 This is my translation of the Russian version reported by Ned Keenan in the 1970s. Later versions substitute 'Jew' for 'Ukrainian bumpkin' (*khokhol*).

POPULAR MUTTERING ABOUT KHRUSHCHEV

For all the security police's vigilance, popular criticism of party leaders was endemic (and we know about it thanks to the police's diligence in recording it). Malicious jokes (*anekdoty*) about leaders  were a staple of many social interactions. Collective male drinking bouts often resulted in acts of desecration, such as cutting up leaders' portraits and flags, throwing ink or vodka at them, spitting at them, and writing anti-Soviet graffiti on busts. The excuse offered, and sometimes even accepted, was 'I was drunk at the time'. No leader, not even Stalin, was immune, but popular mockery of Khrushchev became almost a cottage industry. He was called a 'corn-pedlar' (for his scheme to plant corn in the Virgin Lands), 'comedian', 'trickster', 'the false Tsar Nikita' and even a 'Trotskyite'. 'Khrushchev, you idiot, go away', was one piece of anonymous advice. Mutterers were particularly annoyed by Khrushchev's foreign trips, especially those that involved wooing the Third World, the subject of an urban *skazka* (fairy-tale) of the 1960s:

> Then Nikita started to fly like a bird
> Around foreign countries
> And wherever he went, he gave a gift:
> So-and-so would get a palace,
> Another a little factory,
> Here they got wheat, there a little steamship –
> Thus he robbed his own people
> So that all this other rabble could eat.

Worse was to come on the international scene with the Cuban missile crisis in November 1962. Fidel Castro's pro-Soviet government in Cuba had asked for Soviet military aid against a feared US attack, and Khrushchev secretly sent them some intercontinental nuclear missiles from the Soviet Union's small stockpile. He was not planning to start a war, but intending to deter the Americans from military action, not to mention show them what it felt like 'to have enemy missiles pointed at you [he was thinking of those in Turkey] . . . giving them a little of their own medicine'. US President Kennedy called his bluff, threatening nuclear war if Khrushchev did not back off and have the missiles removed, and after a tense stand-off, Khrushchev complied. To an appalled watching world, it seemed as if superpower competition had taken them to the brink of catastrophe. Khrushchev's Politburo colleagues had the same reaction – plus humiliation that it was the Soviet Union that had blinked, and anger that Khrushchev had got them into the mess in the first place.

Khrushchev's seventieth birthday in April 1964 marked the height of his public cult, but by this point his colleagues were totally fed up with him. Leonid Brezhnev, Khrushchev's protégé, who had had headed the Kazakhstan party committee during the Virgin Lands program and was now back in Moscow as a Politburo member and second secretary of the party, took the lead, quietly lining up Politburo members in support of Khrushchev's dismissal. Vladimir Semichastny of the KGB was in the loop, changing Khrushchev's personal guards as a protection, but it was unneeded insurance. In October, after a two-day discussion in which his colleagues

Khrushchev's grave in Moscow's Novodevichy Cemetery, with bust by
Ernst Neizvestny

criticised his lack of collegiality and errors of judgement, and
Khrushchev, taken aback, made a fumbling response, he was
stripped of his offices by a totally democratic procedure –
a unanimous Politburo vote.

Khrushchev lived out the remaining seven years of his life
as a pensioner in Moscow (a first for a deposed leader) and,
after a period of demoralisation, set to dictating his memoirs. This was perhaps not quite a first, because Trotsky had
done it before him, but unlike Trotsky, Khrushchev remained
loyal, careful not to reveal state secrets, though he was frank
and often funny about his colleagues. As his former speechwriter Fedor Burlatsky later commented, the inflated self-
confidence of his later years in politics was gone, leaving the

peasant commonsense and curiosity. These were still Soviet times, however, so it was obvious that the memoirs couldn't be published at home. The manuscript was smuggled abroad for publication in the United States and became an international bestseller. Soviet politicians avoided Khrushchev in his retirement, but he unexpectedly made friends with some artists and writers who were not afraid to visit. One of them was Neizvestny, the target of Khrushchev's scorn in 1962. The bust that marks Khrushchev's grave in Moscow's Novodevichy Cemetery is his work.

6

THE BREZHNEV PERIOD

THE POLITBURO GOT RID OF KHRUSHCHEV because he had violated the principle of collegiality, so naturally what replaced him had to be a 'collective leadership'. It was headed by a troika: Leonid Brezhnev, organiser of the dismissal, who on Khrushchev's departure became first secretary of the party (and from 1966, general secretary); Aleksei Kosygin heading the Council of Ministers; and Ukrainian Nikolai Podgorny, chairman of the Presidium of the Supreme Soviet. Kosygin was highly visible early on as the promoter of economic reform and building the consumer side of the economy, but his political star waned along with the economic reform during the late 1960s, and by 1977, Podgorny had also been sidelined. Thus it was Brezhnev who won out, ultimately taking over state as well as party leadership and, in his later years, showering himself (or being showered by his colleagues) with honours and decorations, particularly military. It was a long run – almost twenty years – but marred in the five years before his death in 1982 by declining physical and mental capacity, which his increasingly feeble appearance on television made all too visible to the public.

Leonid Brezhnev, born into a Russian working-class family in Ukraine in 1906 and trained as an engineer in the early 1930s, started his political career in the Ukrainian party organisation under Khrushchev, serving as first secretary in Dnepropetrovsk, Moldavia and Kazakhstan before moving to Moscow as a candidate member of the Politburo early in 1956. A cautious pragmatist without intellectual pretensions, he was seen by many as mediocre, and as he became known to the public, he was the butt of many jokes. But he could joke about himself too: when a speechwriter wanted to insert quotations from Marx in one of his public address, he allegedly objected: 'What's the point of that? Who will believe that Lenya Brezhnev has read Marx?' That 'Lenya' (a familiar form of Leonid) was typical of

Leonid Brezhnev as leader, with war decorations (1972)

the man: it was how his Politburo colleagues addressed him, while he in turn called them Yura (Yury Andropov), Kostia (Konstantin Chernenko), Andriusha (Andrei Gromyko) and so on. Vladimir Ilyich (Lenin), Iosif Vissarionovich (Stalin), and even Nikita Sergeevich (Khrushchev), would have felt that was too familiar.

While Brezhnev manoeuvred for primacy among his peers, as Stalin and Khrushchev had done before him, the process was free of bloodletting or even hard landings for those excluded from the inner circle (Brezhnev would usually find them a sinecure lower down the chain, with perks continuing). Despite the minor cult that developed in later years, Brezhnev was basically a much more collegial type than Khrushchev, so that there was a good deal of genuine Politburo collectivity: regular meetings and consultation, no independent 'harebrained schemes', collective decisions, and social and family interactions, often arranged by Brezhnev himself. It was a group that had a lot in common. More than half were of working-class or peasant origin and, like Brezhnev, had been sent to higher education under affirmative action programs, usually studying engineering. As young Communist graduates, they benefited from the very rapid promotion available to that cohort in the wake of the Great Purges. Marxism–Leninism was the ideology they had learned in youth, making state ownership of the means of production a given, along with suspicion of the capitalist West. Much of an age, they had gone through the war together, either in senior government and party positions on the home front or, like Brezhnev, serving as political officers in the armed forces.

The Brezhnev era may have been the best of Soviet times or the most boring, depending on your point of view. But nobody has ever said it was the worst of times, and the Soviet leaders had many causes for satisfaction, particularly in the 1970s before the impact of stalling economic growth rates hit home. This was the period in which the Soviet Union first achieved military parity with the United States and competed with it as an equal for influence in the Third World. It had become a major oil producer, and the price of oil on the international market doubled in the second half of the 1970s, much to the Soviet Union's advantage. The Soviet GNP continued to rise, both absolutely and in relation to other powers, coming the closest it was ever to come to that of the United States in the early 1970s (it was still little more than a third of the US GNP, but in 1946 it had been only a fifth).

Two-thirds of the population were living in towns and cities by the 1980s, compared to a third on the eve of the war. There was no worry about unemployment, and housing rents and prices on basic food goods were kept low. Thanks to the apartment building program started under Khrushchev, the proportion of Soviet families living in separate apartments with their own bathrooms almost doubled in a decade. All the indices of consumer welfare rose: if at the beginning of the 1970s, one in every two families had a TV set and one in every three a refrigerator, by the end of the 1980s there was one of each per family. Private cars – frowned on by Khrushchev – were becoming available, if only for the lucky few. Most rural as well as urban children were now getting a secondary education, while the proportion of the population with higher education more than doubled in the Brezhnev period, reaching just under 10 per cent.

Since the opening of the Soviet borders to tourism abroad in the mid-1950s, hundreds of thousands of Soviet citizens had had a chance to fall in love with Paris, or at least Prague. Life became easier for all groups of the population, particularly in the towns, not only because material circumstances were improving but also because the regime had abandoned the use of random terror and used even targeted measures of repression sparingly.

But this rosy picture needs qualification. The Brezhnev era was not all of a piece, and it was the first decade – the mid-1960s to the mid-1970s – that was the high point. After that it went downhill, particularly with regard to the economy. According to CIA estimates, the growth rate of the Soviet GNP dropped from almost 5 per cent annually in the 1960s to 2–3 per cent in the 1970s and under 2 per cent in the 1980s. High oil prices helped to disguise the problem, but oil prices do not stay high forever. Rising living standards in the 1960s and early '70s generated expectations that rose even faster, encouraged by greater acquaintance with the conditions of life in the West; the result was growing consumer disappointment. Alcoholism, always a problem in the Soviet Union, rose alarmingly, with binge drinking and increased consumption of dubious home-brews contributing to a doubling of the number of deaths from alcohol poisoning in the 1970s. Disturbingly, male life expectancy, which had risen steadily through the Soviet period, started to fall in the mid-1960s, primarily as the result of male alcoholism (women's life expectancy was not affected). It was down from sixty-four in 1965 to sixty-one in 1980, while in the United States over the same period, male life expectancy rose from sixty-seven to seventy.

ABORTIONS

The Soviet Union was the first country to legalise abortion on demand – in 1920, along with other emancipatory measures on women's legal status, marriage and divorce. But its prevalence, along with the instability of marriage attendant upon 'postcard divorce', unsettled traditionally-minded citizens, particularly peasants, and in any case the state was keen to raise birthrates to increase pop-

'Abortion will deprive you of happiness' (1966)
This image was part of a campaign to exercise 'soft' control after the legalisation of abortion.

ulation. In 1936 a draft bill prohibiting abortion was published for public consideration. The lively discussion that ensued was completely different from recent abortion debates in the US and elsewhere, since the issue was not seen either in ethical terms (the right to life) or feminist ones (women's right to control their bodies). Those against abortion usually said it encouraged male fecklessness and promiscuity; others argued that inadequate housing space and/or absent husbands made it a regrettable necessity. Abortion was duly banned from 1936 to 1955, but from the 1950s abortion rates surged again. In the mid 1970s, a key decision was made not to proceed with development of the contraceptive pill in the Soviet Union, and even condoms and IUDs were in very short supply. As a result, surveys in the 1990s showed that three in every four Russian women who had ever been pregnant had had an abortion, some as many as ten. Contraception came in with democracy in post-Soviet Russia, and the number of abortions fell. But despite legal restrictions in recent years, Russia still led the world in abortion rates in 2021.

BARDS OF THE 1960S

Like the United States, the Soviet Union had a 'sixties', though
without the drugs; and, as in the United States, much of the
sixties actually happened in the seventies. In the Soviet Union,

Yuly Kim in performance

bards, singing
their own
songs to the
guitar, were the
spokesmen for a
younger genera-
tion questioning
the authority
of their elders.
Bulat Okudzha-

va's specialty was melancholy and Vladimir Vysotsky's anger,
expressed in the Gulag jargon (*blatnoi iazyk*) that was in vogue
among the young. Yuly Kim, whose Soviet Korean father was executed in the Great Purges, was a bard who later became active in
the dissident movement; he ended up by emigrating to Israel in
1998 with his wife, granddaughter of a purged Jewish Army commander (Iona Yakir). Kim's repertoire in the early '70s included
'The disobedient mother', a setting of a poem from A. A. Milne's
English children's book *Now We are Three*, popular in the Soviet
Union in Samuil Marshak's translation. The eponymous mother
disobeys her young son's orders not to go into town without
him – and disappears. She 'hasn't been heard of since', in Milne's
version, although Marshak softened that by adding a telegram
from the road saying that she was alive and well. Perhaps Kim's
mother was able to send such a message after her arrest, when he
was about three, as the wife of an enemy of the people. He was
nine when she reappeared from Gulag.

Even the successes sometimes had their downsides. All that educational expansion had produced a generational gap of potentially worrying dimensions: by the end of the 1980s, over 90 per cent of people in their twenties had a secondary or higher education, as compared with under 40 per cent of those in their fifties – but it was the latter who were running the country. When US academics compared the results of an interview project with 1970s émigrés with those of the postwar Harvard Interview Project, conducted in the late 1940s, they found that younger interviewees in the 1970s showed less identification with the Soviet Union than their elders did. What their elders welcomed as stability might have seemed more like 'petrification' (to use the term popular with some Western scholars at the time) or 'stagnation' (Mikhail Gorbachev's later characterisation) to the young. 'There in the cemetery it's so

'Vodka specialist': a Kukryniksy poster from the mid-1980s shows a drunken worker passed out at his lathe.

peaceful ... everything cultured and decent ... such a bless-
ing' was the ironical refrain of a song ('*Na kladbishche*') sung at
informal gatherings by the guitar bards of the era.

THE ECONOMY

The biggest long-term problem was the economic system. Central planning, output targets and strong administrative centralisation had worked well as a way of jump-starting a developing
economy in the 1930s. They had performed excellently as a
framework for the wartime economy in the 1940s and had done
a good job of rebuilding industry and infrastructure after the
war. But they were proving much less suitable for the kind of
complex modern economy the Soviet Union needed from the
1960s. The Soviet system proved inhospitable to innovation,
and as the pace of technological change in the world sped up, it
started to lag behind. Foreign technology imports – one example being the 1966 contract with Fiat to build an auto plant in
Togliatti on the Volga – only partially filled the gap. Efficiency
varied sharply between industrial sectors, with the military and
space industries at the top. The productivity of capital investment in industry was very low by world standards, and the
productivity of labour even worse, both in industry and agriculture. Agricultural output grew in the first decade after 1964 but
then went into slightly negative territory, and productivity was
low both in the collective farms and in the state farms, where
workers received a wage. A partial shift away from the collective
farm model and towards large-scale state farms, exemplified in
Khrushchev's Virgin Lands program in Kazakhstan, increased
the sown area but failed to solve the productivity problem.

Having taken advice from reform-minded economists, Kosygin tried to introduce market elements into the planned economy in the mid-1960s, notably by substituting sales (profit) for output as an indicator of enterprise performance. Something like this was tried with considerable success in Hungary under the rubric of the New Economic Mechanism or NEM, evoking memories of the Soviet Union's own market phase in the 1920s, NEP. But in the Soviet Union, where the centralised planning system was more deeply entrenched, reform efforts foundered, largely because of resistance from industrial managers. Enterprises were used to being assessed in terms of gross output, which meant that they had no incentive to improve quality or respond to demand. As economic growth indices started falling in the second half of the 1970s, everybody recognised that there was a problem, but Brezhnev's leadership offered no solution. Perhaps a more radical response would be needed down the line, but meanwhile, why rock the boat? Especially when the Soviet Union was floating along on a sea of oil, with prices for the commodity sky-high.

One of the dirty secrets of the Soviet planned economy was that its functioning depended on a grey market, which effectively, if not wholly legally, moved goods from their producers to the people who needed them. Industrial enterprises participated in this, using agents and cutting deals to get the raw materials they required, and so did ordinary citizens. Friends in the right places helped you get the products and services you needed under the counter. Money sometimes changed hands in these transactions, but the main currency was a running exchange of favours. *Blat* was the term used in the Soviet

Union, the equivalent of *guanxi* in China; Western Sovietologists called it 'the second economy'. It had been in existence since the end of the '20s, largely unnoticed in the West, and this meant that the Soviet Union had actually retained a private sector after the end of NEP, albeit an unofficial one. But its illegality meant it was deeply enmeshed with corruption (bribes and favours to officials were among the methods used to get access to scarce goods) and criminality (the goods sold on the second economy were generally stolen from the first).

By the Brezhnev period, legal access to basic goods had improved. In the meantime, however, consumers had developed a taste for many goods that were *not* necessities, and these desirable goods were always in short supply. Apart from cultivating useful connections, members of the new middle

'Who will beat whom?': Lenin's slogan about class war between the proletariat and the bourgeoisie is put to ironic use in this 1979 cartoon by K. Nevler and M. Ushats on competitive consumption.

class had various ways of getting to the front of the queue. Regional elites had always pushed for special closed-access stores and medical clinics for their own use, sometimes with central approval and sometimes without, but now the numbers of such facilities multiplied, not just for high officials but also for writers, physicists and sportsmen with elite status. Small-scale private businesses run out of the home (dressmaking, electrical work, car repair) flourished more or less legally, as long as there was no hired labour involved. The old Soviet habit persisted of assuming that individual appropriation of state property was something completely different from theft – but now, instead of just picking up bricks and pipes from state construction sites, it might be a matter of siphoning petrol from official limousines into private cars.

'Trust in cadres' was the slogan Brezhnev launched at the Twenty-Third Party Congress in 1966, signalling a central hands-off policy according to which regional and district leaders were generally left to run their own affairs, rarely demoted and, if demoted, not seriously punished. That ensured stability within the bureaucracy, but it also encouraged corruption in ruling elites, which was particularly noticeable in the republics of Central Asia and the Caucasus.

INTERNATIONAL AFFAIRS

The Brezhnev leadership professed a commitment to peace, as indeed had all previous Soviet leaderships, and there was no reason to think it was any less averse to large-scale war than its predecessors – except for its extraordinarily high rate of military spending, which exceeded the levels of previous governments. By 1985, there were almost six million men in the Soviet armed forces, twice as many as in 1960, making them the largest in the world. The defence minister, Marshal Andrei Grechko, was a Politburo member from 1973 – the only military man other than Zhukov, briefly in the mid-1950s, to hold this position. While the old subservient relationship of armed forces to party was basically unchanged, Brezhnev got on well with the military and generally gave them what they wanted.

The post-Khrushchev leadership inherited a tense international situation, with American bases with medium-range nuclear weapons circling the Soviet Union and US politicians expressing alarm about a 'missile gap' to Soviet advantage (although the balance of terror was distinctly on the American side). Berlin was still a flash point, and the outbreak of a third world war seemed to have been narrowly averted in the recent Cuban missile crisis. Reacting to the humiliating backdown over Cuba, the Soviet military argued that a major build-up was needed to be able to stand up to the United States and protect Soviet allies in the future. A 'guns versus butter' debate ensued in the Politburo, but the guns won. US involvement in the war in Vietnam, trying to prop up the failing anti-communist government in the south, rose sharply in the mid-1960s, and tensions were intensified when the Soviet Union started to give military assistance to Ho Chi Minh's North Vietnam in 1965. The US rhetoric had it that Vietnam was a 'domino' whose fall to communism would cause other shaky post-colonial regimes to follow.

But by now, in the wake of the Sino–Soviet split, Soviet pre-eminence in world communism was no longer a given.

The Soviets and the Chinese both supported the north in Vietnam, but China – whose rise in international status was recognised when it took its seat in the UN Security Council in 1971 – was definitely following its own agenda in the Third World, often as much in competition with the Soviet Union as with the United States. In 1969, tensions between the Soviet Union and China over conflicting territorial claims led to armed clashes at the border on the Ussuri River. By the mid-1970s, the Chinese were calling the Soviet Union not only an 'imperialist' power in the Third World but also the more dangerous of the two imperialist superpowers.

Eastern Europe exacerbated Cold War tensions, both because the United States – and its domestic ethnic lobbies – regarded the existence of Soviet-type regimes there as illegitimate and because the populations of these countries inclined towards a similar view. Hungary had issued its challenge and been slapped down in 1956, and the same had happened on a minor scale to Poland in the same year. But in the late 1960s the problem was Czechoslovakia, historically one of the most pro-socialist and pro-Soviet countries in the bloc. When in 1968 a reforming communist leader, Alexander Dubček, tried to introduce 'socialism with a human face' (meaning a reduction of party and police dominance), the Soviet Union sent in tanks. This had damaging repercussions domestically (since it appalled much of the Moscow and Leningrad intelligentsia) and in Eastern Europe, as well as for Soviet relations with the United States. A new 'Brezhnev doctrine' held that the Soviet Union could intervene to save 'socialism' whenever it was threatened, which amounted to an assertion that any country in the Soviet bloc had to stay in it. This was particularly offensive to the Czechs as, unlike the Hungarians in 1956, they had not in fact been seeking to leave the Soviet bloc or abandon socialism – although, had the reforms been implemented, intentions might later have changed.

The Brezhnev regime's military build-up went along, some thought contradictorily, with a search for détente, a relaxation of Cold War tensions, more high-level contacts with the United States and mutual arms-control agreements. There was some progress in this direction in the early 1970s, with an agreement on Berlin signed in 1971 and a strategic arms limitation treaty (SALT I) following the next year. The suave figure of Georgy Arbatov, head of the Soviet USA Institute and earlier one of Khrushchev's advisers, became a familiar presence in the United States, putting the détente case to security experts and, via television, the American public. US hostility towards and suspicion of the Soviet Union ran deep, however, as did its counterpart on the Soviet side, and détente stalled in the second half of the 1970s after America's humiliating withdrawal from Vietnam. The Soviet Union was by now an active competitor with the United States for influence in the Third World, its prestige there raised by its support for the liberation movement in Vietnam, and it backed anti-colonial nationalist forces challenging pro-American governments in Africa, the Middle East and Central America. There were setbacks on both sides in this geopolitical competition: for the Soviets, the Israeli victory over the Arab nations (Egypt, Syria and Jordan) in the Six-Day War of 1967; for the United States, the overthrow of the American-backed Shah of Iran by radical Muslims in 1979.

Soviet foreign policy expert and détente advocate Georgy Arbatov with American Sovietologist Seweryn Bialer

The Six-Day War was a diplomatic defeat for the Soviet Union, but it also created a new domestic problem by stimulating pride and pro-Israeli nationalism among Soviet Jews. This led to a crackdown on 'Zionism' and new restrictions on Jewish cultural life, which in turn sparked a highly visible international campaign for the right of Jews to emigrate. Jewish emigration from the Soviet Union became a human-rights issue that was taken up in the United Nations and the US Congress, leading to the punitive Jackson-Vanik amendment to the US *Trade Reform Act* of 1974. The Soviet leaders were caught in a bind, since they could scarcely defend themselves by arguing (truthfully) that their emigration policies denied this right to *everyone*, not just Jews. In the event, 236,000 Jews left the Soviet Union in the years 1971–1981 (another example of Jewish privilege, in the view of Soviet anti-Semites), slightly over half of them settling in Israel and another large group in the United States. But with many bureaucratic delays and a large exit tax for higher education imposed, the net effect was to underline the Soviet Union's lack of sympathy with Jewish emigration rather than gain any credit for concessions.

More public relations disasters lay in store at the beginning of the 1980s. With the rise of the Solidarity movement in Poland, another threat to communist rule in Eastern Europe presented itself, though this time the Polish government imposed martial law itself and the Soviets got off without having to send in troops. The ill-advised Soviet intervention in defence of a client in Afghanistan's civil war probably owed more to the Brezhnev leadership's idea of how a superpower should behave than any rational analysis of costs and benefits. 'We had to have our own Vietnam,' critics within the Soviet foreign-policy establishment sighed, and so indeed it proved: the Soviet Union, like the United States in Vietnam, accomplished nothing at the cost of many lives and was eventually forced (under Gorbachev) into ignominious retreat. Public disapproval was more low-key than in the American case, but there was similar damage to army morale, and the subsequent Soviet problems with disgruntled and demoralised Afghanistan war veterans were probably even worse than those the United States had with its Vietnam vets.

Afghanistan notwithstanding, Brezhnev's Soviet Union could congratulate itself on avoiding the alarming instability of the other superpower. The United States lurched through waves of student and civil-rights unrest in the 1960s, anti-Vietnam protests and Black Panthers, to a major crisis of government legitimacy in the Watergate affair, leading to the impeachment of President Nixon and his resignation in August 1974. Thank goodness Soviet national minorities were not as angry and mutinous as black Americans, and Soviet young people not so alienated from their elders and contemptuous of social decorum as their American counterparts, Brezhnev and many Soviet citizens must have thought – and what did Americans have to complain about anyway, with their huge suburban houses, double martinis and fancy cars?

IN THE REPUBLICS

It was certainly true that the Soviet Union had nothing like the American race problem with its national minorities. Overt ethnic conflicts were comparatively rare, and when they occurred were as likely to be between two ethnic minorities, or an ethnic minority and the titular majority in one of the Central Asian or Caucasian republics, as to involve Russians. The ethnic deportations of the 1940s had created problems, including in Kazakhstan, where the republican leadership's unhappiness at being landed with the newcomers was almost as strong as the newcomers' distress at being landed there. There were more problems when some of the 'banished peoples' were able to return to their former homes after Khrushchev's Secret Speech, only to find them occupied by strangers. The Baltic republics were still resentful at being incorporated into the Soviet Union in 1939 – an 'eastern', hence culturally inferior power, in the Baltic view – and thus losing their interwar independence. Strong passive anti-Russian feeling persisted throughout the region, and in Lithuania a nationalist protest movement centred on the Catholic church had an underground existence from the early 1970s.

Friendship of nations is celebrated in this 1979 cartoon by Iu Cherepanov, marking the 325th anniversary of 'Ukraine's Union with Russia' under the Treaty of Pereyaslav.

The republics were increasingly led by locals, drawing on the support of indigenous elites and presenting themselves in national (and, in Central Asia, secular Islamic) colours. After Kazakh Dinmukhamed Kunaev was named first secretary of Kazakhstan in October 1964 (following a series of Russian and Ukrainian first secretaries, including Brezhnev, during the Virgin Lands period), the enrolment of ethnic Kazakhs in the party doubled in two years. As before, there was generally a Slavic second secretary acting as Moscow's eyes and ears in the republics, but in the Brezhnev period, when Kunaev and Volodymyr Shcherbytsky were full members of the Politburo, and the Azerbaijani, Georgian, Uzbek and Belorussian first secretaries were candidate members, these local second secretaries were clearly outranked. The republican leaders were energetic (and mutually competitive) lobbyists for Moscow investment, and most of them were net beneficiaries in the economic flow of resources. The Baltics, the most developed part of the Soviet Union with the highest per capita incomes, were the exception, contributing, along with the Russian Republic and Ukraine, to the subsidy of less-developed republics.

While the official long-term plan was to merge national differences, there were few signs that this was happening. Rather, the republics, with Moscow's tacit agreement, were quietly asserting and consolidating national particularity. In questionnaires, Soviet citizens strongly endorsed ethnic tolerance, but in practice they had an equally strong preference for marrying within their own ethnic group, or at least one closely akin (Russian and Belorussian, Uzbek and Tajik). Intermarriage rates were low, and such intermarriage as occurred was often between people already living outside their native republics. Given the much higher birth rates in the Muslim areas of the Soviet Union (the Central Asian republics and Azerbaijan) than in the historically Christian regions (Russia, Ukraine, Belorussia, Armenia, Georgia), demographers started to see a future in which Slavs would be in the minority.

Indeed, it could have seemed that the major nationality problem of the Brezhnev era was actually a Russian one. Russian may have been the lingua franca of the Soviet Union, and Moscow its capital, but Russians were the ethnic group that had traditionally received least encouragement for displays of national culture and the fostering of national pride and culture. In literature, a quasi-nationalist trend developed, focusing primarily on the Russian village, and in the social realm, emerging movements to preserve historical monuments and combat industrial degradation of the environment acquired a distinctly nationalist tinge (Russophile writer Valentin Rasputin was one of those who became deeply involved in the movement to save Siberia's Lake Baikal). Future Gorbachev adviser Aleksandr Yakovlev found himself in trouble for criticising Russian nationalist sympathisers within the Central Committee bureaucracy in the early 1970s, and it was rumoured that they had patrons even in the Politburo. In the non-Slavic regions, particularly Central Asia, the policy of supporting indigenous promotion had come at the expense of local Russian residents, who were starting to feel less at home. Among Russians, the sense of carrying out a virtuous civilising mission in the less-developed regions of the Soviet Union was giving way to a degree of resentment based on the perception that their republic was subsidising the weaker ones at the expense of its own citizens – in short, that the non-Slavic republics were a burden on Russia rather than an asset.

The Slavic regions of the country were experiencing a generational gap that was less dramatic than what existed in the contemporary United States but in some ways resembled it. There was a 'sixties' generation in the Soviet Union too, exchanging Beatles tapes to play in their new tape recorders, wearing blue jeans made in Eastern Europe, spicing up their vocabulary with Gulag jargon, singing Vladimir Vysotsky's songs on their guitars and listening to foreign radio (the 'Voices'). By the 1970s, rock music was the big attraction, flourishing even in Komsomol circles, despite moderate official disapproval. Perhaps more worrying for Communist true

believers was the political passivity of the younger generation, compared with its prewar precursors. As portrayed by
participant-observer Alexei Yurchak, the youth of the 1970s
and '80s accepted official language and rituals, and performed
them fluently, but regarded their 'real' lives as being lived in a
private sphere on which the public sphere barely impinged.
By Soviet standards, their educational levels were spectacular,
and with full employment they had no worries about getting
a job – although for university graduates there was plenty of
worry about whether the assigned job would be in Moscow or
in the boondocks.

DAILY LIFE OF SOVIET CITIZENS

'We pretend to work and they pretend to pay us' was a joke
that was even more popular with Western journalists than in
the Soviet Union. But the Soviet workplace had advantages
beyond tolerance of low productivity, as its denizens discovered when the Soviet Union collapsed. The workplace, with
its special onsite shops and buffets, was a source of scarce
goods for its employees (how good a source depended on the
state and prestige of the plant, industrial sector or ministry) and an arena of camaraderie. Many pleasant hours were
spent by women drinking tea with cake with office colleagues,
and by men sharing a companionable cigarette (or even a
companionable vodka) in the stairwell. If the economists had
been trying to measure happiness at work instead of labour
productivity, they might have come up with better results.

The Brezhnev years were good ones for ordinary Soviet
citizens: it was at this time that the promises of universal

'welfare state' protection, made from the earliest days of Soviet rule, were fully realised. The guaranteed minimum wage, first introduced in 1956, was raised, as were pensions, which Soviet citizens could receive at the early ages of sixty for men and fifty-five for women. Welfare benefits previously confined to wage-earners were extended to kolkhozniks. In a surprising trend for a recently developed country, social differentiation diminished and a generally egalitarian ethos prevailed. This was often overlooked in the West, where commentators liked to make much of the fact that there was inequality under socialism and bosses had privileges. Of course there was inequality, and naturally the Soviets tried to pretend there wasn't. But on an international comparative scale, it was relatively minor and not trending upwards.

For the Soviet Union's middle class, there was not too much privilege but too little; and this middle class was growing spectacularly. If in 1941 there had been 2.4 million people with higher or secondary education, by 1960 the number was up to eight million, and by the end of the 1980s thirty-two million. Many of these people would, as a matter of course, join the Communist Party, whose numbers continued to rise, reaching close to sixteen million by 1976. The privileges that these people valued and hoped for included a dacha in the countryside as well as their small urban apartments, the new possibility of purchasing a 'cooperative apartment' for grown-up children, foreign travel, some access to foreign luxury goods and a car. There were still not enough of such coveted goods to go round, and not enough jobs that carried the salary and status that would procure them. Many high-school graduates in white-collar jobs were on a salary of 500 roubles, while a blue-collar worker might earn 300 roubles. When the postwar rise in the overall standard of living slowed in the 1970s and 1980s, there were ample grounds for an undertow of dissatisfaction among those whose expectations had risen so dramatically in previous decades.

In the intelligentsia, there was a sense of malaise. The heady optimism of the Khrushchev period was gone, with the 1968 intervention in Czechoslovakia marking the watershed. Intellectuals' hopes of spiritual leadership were dashed, and they felt society was becoming increasingly materialistic. Those with material aspirations were also frustrated. In the diagnosis of American observer John Bushnell, the Soviet citizen had become a pessimist, listening to the mournful songs of Bulat Okudzhava and telling slightly politically risqué but also self-mocking jokes like this one, set in a political literacy (civics) class:

(*Questioner*:) 'Is there life on the moon?'

(*Instructor*:) 'No, comrade, Soviet cosmonauts have found no signs of life on the moon.'

(*Questioner*, sadly:) 'Not there either?'

For all the cultivation of private life that was characteristic of the era, an embryonic associational life was emerging, separate from the state and focused mainly on protecting the natural environment and preserving historical and cultural monuments. These were generally 'liberal' preoccupations, but on the non-liberal and potentially nationalist side, ex-soldiers had finally managed to get permission to create veterans' organisations, which were of great importance to the generation of men who had fought in World War II and kept up informal contact with their units through regular heavy-drinking reunions over the years. The 'thick' journals that had flourished during the Khrushchev era were still around, though most had endured a change of editor and greater restrictions on political, especially anti-Stalinist, content. *Oktiabr*, *Novy Mir*'s conservative competitor, had a *succès de scandale* with Vsevolod Kochetov's *So What Do You Want?*, which attacked corrupting Western influences in a spirit of Stalinist nostalgia. A growing competitor to the thick journals was *samizdat* – self-published, and therefore uncensored, manuscripts on various touchy topics, from politics to religion to yoga, copied on typewriters and circulated by hand. A smaller relative, *tamizdat*, circulated banned literature brought in from the West.

By the 1980s, rates of female education and workforce participation were spectacular. The number of women wage- and salary-earners tripled, from twenty million in 1960 to almost sixty million in 1989, when they constituted 50.6 per cent of the workforce. In the whole Soviet population aged ten years and over, as of 1979, 60 per cent of women had secondary or higher education (for men it was 69 per cent) – and this high rate prevailed even in Uzbekistan, one of the republics where women had historically been most disadvantaged. Women were entering the party in greater numbers than ever before, composing 25 per cent of members in 1976 and 30 per cent in

1990. But the double burden of a full-time job plus shopping, housework and child rearing (all 'women's work') was taking its toll, as Natalia Baranskaya vividly described in a novella published in *Novy Mir*, 'A Week like any Other' – without explicitly mentioning the problems associated with the unavailability of the contraceptive pill, which would have been too much for the prudish censor. For all the state provision of creches and kindergartens, the lives of working Soviet women were truly manageable only with a non-working *babushka* (grandmother) in residence.

The West was a powerful presence in the Soviet Union, not just as bogeyman but as cultural magnet. Half of the working population of Moscow listened to Western radio stations, according to a survey; young men called each other Alec and Mike instead of Sasha and Misha. By the 1980s, even middle-aged men might be seen of a weekend in jeans and black leather jackets, driving their cars (joyously but badly, since they were late learners) to the dacha. There, after Donald Kendall's pioneering deal trading Pepsi for Stolichnaya vodka, they would drink both in alternation, the bottle of Pepsi on the kitchen table symbolising cosmopolitan savoir vivre. In Western Sovietological circles, it was for a time fashionable to talk about 'convergence', a theory built on the assumption that with modernisation, Soviet society would inevitably get more liberal, democratic, individualistic and pluralistic – in short, more like Western society. That sounded good to many in the Soviet Union, although the convergence they were mainly interested in was a convergence in the availability of Western-style products.

THE DISSIDENTS

Western connections were important for a new phenomenon on the Soviet scene: the dissident movement. Samizdat and tamizdat, combined with the feedback loop of Western radio, made it possible for 'non-standard thinkers' (*inakomysliashchie*) to get their thoughts into circulation in the Soviet Union, as well as build an audience and support group abroad. Initially, the urge to express non-standard ideas did not necessarily imply opposition to the Soviet Union, but after the satirical writers Andrei Sinyavsky and Yuly Daniel were put on public trial in 1966 and convicted of 'anti-Soviet propaganda' for publishing their work abroad, the two started to merge. Further impetus to the dissident movement was given by the Soviet intervention in Czechoslovakia, when many intellectuals signed protests against the invasion and found themselves with black marks in their personnel files as a result.

After serving a sentence in Gulag, Sinyavsky was allowed to emigrate to France, and this became the preferred way of dealing with literary dissidents, though some were committed to mental hospitals on the presumption that anyone who gratuitously put himself out on a limb by insisting on his own unpopular opinion had to be crazy. Russian-Jewish poet Joseph Brodsky, sentenced under Khrushchev's 'anti-parasite' law in 1964, was invited by the KGB to emigrate in 1971 and, when he demurred, was peremptorily put on a plane to Vienna and deported in 1972. Aleksandr Solzhenitsyn's Soviet citizenship was revoked in 1974 and he was flown, against his will, to Europe. In terms of the international reputation of the Soviet Union, it was a dubious strategy, since the exiled dissidents, now with the halo of martyrdom, continued to publish their criticisms for the benefit of a receptive Western audience. Soviet discomfiture was compounded by a spate of much-publicised defections, including Stalin's unhappy daughter, Svetlana, and the dancer Rudolph Nureyev in 1967.

The dissidents' political positions ranged from more or less disillusioned Communists like the Medvedev twins, Zhores and Roy, to liberals like Andrei Sakharov (distinguished physicist and member of the Academy of Sciences, exiled in 1980 to the city of Gorky on the Volga) and Russophile conservatives, as Solzhenitsyn ultimately became. The thread that united them was advocacy of human rights and the use of Western media as a platform. Foreign correspondents in Moscow were the dissidents' lifeline, providing friendship as well as Johnnie Walker whisky and Marlboro cigarettes, smuggling out their work and, when they got into trouble, making their cases front-page news in Europe and North America. The CIA and other Western intelligence agencies also provided quiet indirect support, not necessarily requested or even known by the recipients, but emphasised in Soviet media attacks on them. Not surprisingly, this did not make the dissidents popular with ordinary citizens in the Soviet Union, and, except in the case of nationalist dissidence, the movement made little contact with the broader Soviet public. In the popular seditious materials the KGB regularly collected (mainly irreverent rhymes, obscenities and jokes, complaints about shortages and price rises and drunken denunciations of leaders), the dissidents whose names were so well known in the West go virtually unmentioned.

Over time, nevertheless, the dissident critique, combined with memories of Khrushchev's denunciation of Stalinism in 1956, sank in and diffused through the elite, first the younger generation and then their parents. By the 1980s, solid Soviet citizens with good jobs might scoff at the dissidents when talking to foreigners, even off the record, while at the same time making criticisms of the Soviet life that they would never have voiced twenty years earlier.

It was so rare in the early 1980s to encounter anyone who professed fervent support for the Soviet Union and took its ideology seriously that many people assumed that the old utopian revolutionary spirit had had its last hurrah under Khrushchev. But this may have been too sweeping.

Non-conformist Ukrainian-Armenian artist Vagrich Bakhchanyan's take on Mukhina's statue was made soon after his emigration to the United States in 1974.

Evtushenko, the most famous of the public poets of the Thaw, accustomed to being viewed as a troublemaker in the 1970s, suddenly in the 1980s started encountering younger bureaucrats with nostalgic memories of smuggling their way into his poetry readings when they were students twenty years earlier. And it wasn't only the '60s generation whose youthful idealism was hidden behind a workaday Brezhnevian facade. In the 1950s, Moscow University had already been producing idealists. One of them, Mikhail Gorbachev, had made his way up the party ladder to first secretary in Stavropol and was back in Moscow – waiting, though he didn't know it yet, to start the revolution that would destroy the Soviet Union.

7

THE FALL

IT WAS CAPITALISM THAT WAS BOUND to collapse, according to Marxist theory, not socialism. That made it all the more unimaginable to Soviet leaders and citizens that the opposite could happen – and particularly that it could happen without the United States cheating by dropping nuclear bombs on the competition. Socialism had history on its side, until suddenly and seemingly inexplicably, history went haywire. As in the evocative title of Alexei Yurchak's study of late Soviet socialism, 'Everything was forever until it was no more'.

Even optimists among American Sovietologists had not seriously predicted the collapse of the Soviet Union: such a regime would not fall without overwhelming external or domestic pressures for the simple reason that its powerful army and police would prevent this. Similarly, it was inconceivable that any Soviet government would give away control over Eastern Europe unless militarily defeated, still less to allow secession of the non-Russian republics. When the impossible happened, and moreover in the absence of major popular uprisings in either the Soviet Union or Eastern Europe that would have stretched, let alone defeated, Soviet security capacities, it inflicted a trauma on the Russians that has few equals, even in the trauma-filled twentieth century. Defeat in World War II shocked the Germans, and revelations about the Holocaust left them with a massive task of *Vergangenheitsbewältigung* (coming to terms with the past) – but still, it was comprehensible as a defeat in war, with German armies fighting bravely to the last. For the Soviet Union, the collapse came suddenly out of the unravelling of Mikhail Gorbachev's ambitious reform program, unopposed and with no apparent necessity or historical logic to justify it.

A century and a half earlier, in his classic *The Old Regime and the French Revolution*, Alexis de Tocqueville had suggested that 'the most dangerous moment for a bad government is generally that in which its sets about reform'. But that would have been cold comfort for Gorbachev, who thought of himself as revitalising a revolution, not salvaging an 'old regime'.

GORBACHEV AND DOMESTIC REFORM

Brezhnev was in his mid-seventies at the beginning of the '80s, but he had seemed old and sick for years. The men around him, gathered in a protective phalanx in his last years, were old too. When he finally died in 1982, they turned to Yury Andropov, the KGB head, eight years younger than Brezhnev but much livelier, with a stable of reform-minded young thinkers like Fedor Burlatsky around him. But after little more than a year Andropov quickly took sick and died as well, to be succeeded by an undistinguished Brezhnev protégé, Konstantin Chernenko, who lasted for about the same length of time before dying in his turn. At this point, even the old guard had to concede that they needed a younger man at the head of the party. The choice fell on Mikhail Gorbachev, twenty years younger than Chernenko and twenty-five years younger than Brezhnev. He had been brought to Moscow in 1978 to take charge of agriculture nationally after twenty years running the party in Stavropol, an agricultural region, where he was born. A Politburo member since 1980, Gorbachev had been Andropov's choice of successor (passed over in favour of the senior Chernenko by Politburo colleagues) in 1984. He became general secretary of the party in March 1985.

Gorbachev was open-minded and energetic, a good politician and consensus-builder, and an effective administrator

Fedor Burlatsky (in the centre), a reform advocate and policy adviser under Khrushchev, Andropov and Gorbachev, with American Sovietologist Jerry Hough

who knew the country outside Moscow, but in the early 1980s he scarcely looked like a future revolutionary. A beneficiary of upward mobility, though of later vintage than Khrushchev and Brezhnev, he came from a peasant family that had suffered in a number of familiar ways in the Stalin period, with two uncles and an aunt dying in the famine of the early '30s and both grandfathers arrested during the Great Purges. (Such contradictory biographies were not unusual in his generation; his colleague and later opponent Boris Yeltsin's biography was similar, as was that of the Georgian who would later became his foreign minister, Eduard Shevardnadze.) Too young to fight in World War II, Gorbachev lacked the central experience around which the Brezhnev leadership bonded. A lawyer, not an engineer, by training, he was the first Soviet leader to think of himself as a member of the intelligentsia, an identity equally important to his wife, Raisa, a sociologist. He recognised that he was 'a product of the system', while also categorising himself as 'a man of the '60s'. A serious reader of Lenin, he was nevertheless silently critical of the Soviet invasion of Czechoslovakia in 1968 and regretful that, in the aftermath, the Soviet Union had turned away from the path of internal reform.

Gorbachev saw reform through the prism of the Thaw, as a revitalisation of socialism rather than an abandonment of it. His two watchwords, announced at the Twenty-Seventh Party Congress early in 1986, were *perestroika* (rebuilding) and *glasnost* (openness and transparency). Of these, Gorbachev ended up putting glasnost first, the better to work out how to rebuild. It was the opposite of the choice made in Deng

Xiaoping's China (still in a state of estrangement from the Soviet Union) at around the same time, and Deng was said by his son to have thought Gorbachev 'an idiot' for not putting economic reform ahead of political. That seems a fair verdict in retrospect, given the comparative outcomes of Soviet and Chinese reforms, but Gorbachev's reasoning also made some sense at the time: he knew very well how strong the entrenched forces against economic reorganisation could be (remember Khrushchev's regional economic councils!) and hoped to overcome them with the help of a public opinion headed by a reform-minded intelligentsia.

Glasnost hit the Soviet public before any significant perestroika was felt. That was in line with the intelligentsia's assumption that reform meant, first and foremost, the lifting of impediments to free discussion. Names from the 1960s – such as Evgeny Evtushenko, who would be a Gorbachev supporter to the Congress of People's Deputies in 1989, and Vladimir Dudintsev, with a new anti-Lysenko novel, *Robed in White* – emerged out of the shadows back into celebrity, and Solzhenitsyn's *Gulag Archipelago* and George Orwell's *1984* were published in the Soviet Union for the first time. De-Stalinization resumed; Bukharin and Zinoviev were rehabilitated, along with the Workers' Opposition of the early 1920s and the Jewish doctors condemned in the 1952 'doctors' plot'; even Trotsky, though never rehabilitated, became mentionable again.

Everything the intelligentsia had ever hoped for in terms of freedom of expression and publication was suddenly available. Thanks to glasnost, the Soviet press was full of informed, detailed criticisms of historical 'mistakes' such as collectivisation, the

Great Purges, bad decisions in World War II, wartime ethnic deportations and postwar anti-Semitism. Newspapers and thick journals competed with each other for exposés, publishing all the manuscripts in drawers that had hitherto been forbidden and pushing for rehabilitation of fallen revolutionary heroes. It was a wonderful time to be a Soviet writer of a certain age and type – a Khrushchevian truth-teller whose realist novels and plays unmasked social ills, historical cover-ups and political scandals. It was an equally exciting time to be a Soviet reader, except that there was too much to read, and what one read was likely to shake one's faith in the Soviet system. Gorbachev's assumption, like that of the old reform-minded thick journals, was that 'telling the truth' could not but be good, ultimately strengthening the Soviet system by purifying it. Unfortunately, the opposite proved to be the case. The effect of the crash course on the flaws of Soviet socialism was to undermine the public's confidence rather than rally it for reform.

Gorbachev's reforms started off on a puritanical note with a crackdown on vodka. This took up a theme from Andropov's short period of rule and made sense as a response to falling male life expectancy and low labour productivity. But it was bad for the state budget and very unpopular with drinkers, that is to say with the great majority of Slavic men. With regard to economic reform, Gorbachev proceeded with extreme caution. Cooperatives – since Lenin, a standard Soviet response to problems of bureaucratic centralisation that had never worked any magic before – were his first proposal. Since the co-op members could employ labour as long as they themselves worked, these had the potential to function as private businesses, but their establishment was hedged round with restrictions and plagued by unanswered questions such as what premises a fledgling cooperative might use in the absence of a commercial real-estate market. Similar problems attended legislation that allowed peasants to set up their own farms but maintained the existing prohibition on the buying and selling of land. Joint ventures with foreign investors were allowed from 1987, but negotiating Soviet bureaucracy and establishing reliable supply sources proved extremely difficult for the foreigners. McDonald's was the big success story when it finally opened its first outlet in Moscow in 1990. But behind that success lay more than a decade of careful preparation, including growing its own potatoes for the fries, rearing its

'Good Sir, wouldn't you like an American Big Mac?': a 1991 cartoon by V. Polukhin

own cattle for the hamburgers and teaching its Russian staff to smile at customers instead of scowling.

Gorbachev's suspicion of the market was one factor hampering economic reform. But there were also solid political reasons for proceeding slowly. The Soviet population had got used to heavily subsidised prices on basic goods, but any move in a market direction was bound to see them rise. The Soviet welfare state, prized by its citizens, was closely linked with delivery of goods and services at the (state-owned) workplace, another issue that would be complex to solve under privatisation.

The Chernobyl disaster in April 1986 served as a catalyst for the launching of glasnost, particularly in the form of criticism of high-ranking officials and public awareness of environmental hazards. As luck would have it, 1986 was the year that oil prices started going down from their historic highs of the 1970s and early '80s. Having risen from around US$60 a barrel in the mid-1970s to over US$120 in 1980, they dropped precipitously from the end of 1985 and stayed down in the US$40 range for the rest of the decade. Annual growth of Soviet GNP was less than half what it had been under Khrushchev, and it fell to minus 2.3 per cent in 1990. Surveying the Soviet economic situation in his report to the Central Committee in June 1987, Gorbachev said that waste, inefficiency and inaccurate reporting had created a 'pre-crisis' situation.

Demographically, the outlook, if not critical, was somewhat gloomy. Women, both urban and rural, were having fewer children outside the Muslim areas of the country, and Russians were declining as a proportion of the total population, reaching 50.7 per cent by 1989 (had the Soviet Union survived until the next scheduled census date, they would have dropped below 50 per cent for the first time). Male life expectancy had pulled up a little after the alarming decline of the 1970s, with men gaining a year and a half in the 1980s, but it was still eight years short of an average American life span. Despite this, it was an aging population, with almost as many pensioners (thirty million) as there were members of the Komsomol youth organisation.

In terms of political strategy, Gorbachev, known as a skilled negotiator and conciliator, showed these skills in dealing with the renovation of the Politburo, persuading some of the older Politburo veterans to retire more or less gracefully. Among the new blood he brought in was Boris Yeltsin, arriving from the Urals to head the Moscow party organisation late in 1985, who soon emerged as the Politburo's radical hothead, resigning dramatically in 1987 after clashing with Politburo conservatives. Gorbachev never succeeded in building a united Politburo that was firmly committed to reform under his leadership, partly because of continuing uncertainty as to what kind of reform he had in mind. He came to rely more on reform-minded advisers not previously in the inner circle such as Aleksandr Yakovlev, a party liberal who, as head of the Central Committee's propaganda department, had appointed reformers to key positions in the media. After his promotion to the Politburo in 1987, Yakovlev became a lightning rod for criticism from hardliners.

If Gorbachev moved carefully with the Politburo, he was much tougher in his approach to republican and regional first secretaries, the great majority of whom were replaced in short order. Although, like Khrushchev and Brezhnev, Gorbachev was a former regional secretary himself, he lacked his predecessors' sense of the importance of support from this political constituency. Nor did he show much sensitivity to national concerns: among the Central Asian leaders removed in an attempt to clean up corruption was Dinmukhamed Kunaev, who was replaced as first secretary of Kazakhstan by a Russian. (This provoked rioting in Alma-Ata, and after a few years the Russian was replaced by a Kazakh.)

In 1987, Gorbachev added 'democratisation' (*demokratizatsiia*) to his reform goals. Although a Western word and concept, something like democratisation had its own history in the Soviet context, harking back to experiments with multi-candidate elections for soviet deputies and party officials in the mid-1920s, and then again in the mid-1930s. These had failed in the past, quietly and without disastrous consequences. If they were to fail again, it might be possible to take the more radical step of allowing the development of policy-based factions within the ruling Communist Party (something that hadn't even been discussed since the early 1920s) or, more radical yet, to allow the formation of opposition parties, abolishing the 'leading role' that made the Communist Party the only legal arena of politics. But Gorbachev was far from thinking in those terms in the early stages of perestroika. The 'democratisation' he outlined at the Nineteenth Party Conference in June 1988 involved shifting executive authority from the party to state authorities (once known as 'revitalisation of the soviets') and allowing multi-candidate elections.

But there was also a surprise: Gorbachev's announcement that elections would be held for an institution without historical precedent, a Congress of People's Deputies, whose purpose was to elect a new Supreme Soviet that would become the engine of perestroika. In contrast to the familiar pattern of soviet elections, where a single candidate (nominated, in effect, by the Communist Party) was put up for popular vote, here there were to be multiple candidates, and much of the political excitement lay in their selection. The Communist Party still had a bloc of seats allocated for its nominations, but so did a range of other 'social organisations', including the trade unions, women's councils (a throwback to an organisational form largely neglected since the 1920s), the Writers' Union and the Academy of Sciences. The Communist Party's nomination process was sedate, the main drama being the exclusion from its list of troublemaker Boris Yeltsin (who was nominated for one of the Moscow seats anyway, running against the official party candidate and trouncing him with 89 per cent of the popular vote). But in the Academy of Sciences and the Writers' Union, there was high drama around the selection process, as reformers and conservatives competed for places.

The election, held in March 1989, resulted in a congress in which 85 per cent of the 2250 deputies were Communists (not surprisingly, in a society where party membership was the norm for educated and ambitious citizens), but 20 per cent of candidates actually put up by the party were defeated, and the elected deputies included a solid group of radicals, including Yeltsin and dissident Andrei Sakharov, who, after the congress met, did their best to organise themselves into a voting bloc. Most of the reform-minded deputies were from the intelligentsia, but the intelligentsia contingent also contained Slavophile nationalists such as the writer Valentin Rasputin. Ordinary workers, collective farmers and women – categories for whom places had always been kept in the old undemocratic single-candidate soviet elections – were poorly represented in the new congress compared to the old Supreme Soviet, having been much less energised by glasnost than the intelligentsia. But non-Russian nationalities, the other traditional beneficiary of undemocratic nomination practices in the past, were beginning to find political voices. 'Popular fronts', initially combining reform supporters and nationalists, had emerged in the Baltic states, and their support was crucial to candidates' success in the elections. Among an unexpectedly large number of defeats for senior party candidates, even those running unopposed, were the prime ministers of Latvia and Lithuania and the party's first secretaries of five republican capitals, including Kiev.

Glasnost had created an essentially free press, with major outlets committed to the reform cause, and when the congress met, its televised proceedings beamed passionate attacks on Gorbachev's policy from Yeltsin and Sakharov across the country. So-called 'informal associations' were springing up all over the country, most of them small, catering to a host of interests and causes, from ecology to weightlifting. In terms of political tendencies, they ran the gamut from liberal and social democratic to varieties of nationalism. The 'Memorial' society, founded by former dissidents in January 1989, was a human-rights organisation supporting victims of repression. On the other side of the political spectrum, 'Pamyat' (memory) was committed to national regeneration in a spirit of Orthodoxy, with some anti-Semitism thrown in. Within the 'popular fronts', which had spread from the Baltics to other republics, the original (pro-perestroika) reform component was often swamped by nationalist enthusiasm that was increasingly unresponsive to any kind of leadership from Moscow, including in the service of reform.

Republican elections held under the new rules began in the last months of 1989 and continued through the spring of 1990. Apart from the Communist Party, there were still no organised political parties, but there were ad hoc political 'groups' and 'blocs' putting up slates of candidates, and from the party's standpoint the results were increasingly alarming. Estonia's elections, the first in the series, produced a republican parliament in which the local popular front and its allies outnumbered Communist Party nominees and provided the new prime minister. In Georgia, voting last of the republics in October 1990, the Communist Party, with 30 per cent of the vote, lost outright to a nationalist coalition with 54 per cent. At the elections in between, nationalists from the 'Rukh' organisation and the 'Greens' won a large number of seats, with the successful candidates from the Western Ukraine including a metropolitan of the Orthodox Church. In Russia, a reform group ('Democratic Russia') won many seats in the larger cities and got over a fifth of the vote in the republic as a whole; after some wrangling, its candidate, Yeltsin, was elected chairman of the republican Supreme Soviet (now often referred to as a 'parliament' in Western reports). Only in Central Asia were the local ruling Communist elites still firmly in charge of the process, often putting up only one (successful) candidate.

There had been some attempts to pluralise the political process by organising factions (the Democratic and Marxist 'platforms') within the Communist Party itself, but these came to nothing, and it became clear that the spontaneous pluralisation underway was going to take place outside and against the Communist Party. Reform-minded Communists, accordingly, started to quit the party. It had been no part of Gorbachev's original intention to create a multi-party system in the Soviet Union or to abolish the Communist Party's 'leading role', but under pressure, he had to concede both early in 1990. It wasn't until October that this was formalised

'Glory to the Communist Party of the Soviet Union', the old triumphalist slogan, is being furtively painted on a wall by someone who looks like a petty bureaucrat in this 1990 cartoon by Iu Cherepanov.

by a law on public association, but rudimentary parties were already proliferating – anarchist, monarchist, 'national-patriotic', liberal, social democratic, even an 'Idiots' Party' offering beer and sausages. A Russian Communist Party was allowed for the first time to hive off from the Soviet one in June and proved to be dominated by hardliners. As a result, the exodus of reformers from the Communist Party intensified, with Yeltsin and the reform-minded mayors of Moscow and Leningrad (Gavriil Popov and former law professor Anatoly Sobchak) resigning demonstratively in July. By the middle of 1991, the party had lost over four million members, shrinking by 25 per cent.

Gorbachev himself was still a member, with a power base in the party through his position as its general secretary. But with the Communist Party increasingly occupying (or at least seen to be occupying) the anti-reform position, the situation was increasingly untenable for a reforming leader. In March 1990, the Congress of People's Deputies elected him to the new office of president of the Soviet Union. The Soviet Union had had formal heads of state before (party elder Mikhail Kalinin held that position in the 1920s and '30s), but they were not given the title of *prezident* (a Western borrowing) and did not play an executive role. Gorbachev's would be the first and last executive presidency for the Soviet Union. The trouble was, the office came without an established power base and executive apparatus, leaving Gorbachev – not a popularly elected president, as his election had come from the congress – to operate with the support of a discredited Communist Party and a contentious parliament (the Supreme Soviet).

LAST SURVIVORS

After years of fruitless trying, Vyacheslav Molotov was readmitted to the Communist Party in 1984 (he had been expelled over twenty years earlier as part of the 'Anti-Party group'). He thus became the oldest living party member, having joined in 1906. It was a sweet moment of vindication not offered to his colleague

Molotov with the journalist Felix Chuev in the 1980s; Stalin's portrait is behind them.

Lazar Kaganovich, who tried equally hard for reinstatment but was turned down (a whiff of anti-semitism on the part of Chernenko's Politburo?), albeit with the possibility of reconsideration. Dying at the age of 96 in November 1986, Molotov lived long enough to see the beginning of Gorbachev's *perestroika* but not the end. Felix Chuev, who interviewed Molotov extensively in his last decades, reported temperately favourable first reactions to the anti-alcohol campaign and the reform programme mooted at the 27th Party Congress: Brezhnev had let things slide, Molotov thought, and at least the new youngster showed 'a desire to struggle for socialism'. Outliving Molotov, Kaganovich was still around to see the unravelling of *perestroika* and the party in 1990-91. The harsh attacks of radical critics at

Kaganovich towards the end of the 1980s, wearing the 'Hero of the Soviet Union' medal.

the Soviet Communist party's 28th (and last) congress in July 1990 were 'shameful', he told Chuev indignantly: delegates were calling the Soviet Union 'totalitarian' and talking about Soviet life as a 'kind of slavery', just what Western enemies had been saying for 70 years. Lonely and embittered, the last surviving member of Stalin's Politburo, Kaganovich died at 97 on 25 July 1991 – only five months before the dissolution of the Soviet Union.

FOREIGN RELATIONS

Given the evolving domestic situation, it is scarcely surprising that Gorbachev, who excelled in foreign relations and had great success in dealing with Western leaders, reacted to the adulation of adoring crowds on the streets of Western capitals ('Gorby, Gorby!') by focusing more and more attention there. What he saw as his big task, like Brezhnev before him, was to come to terms with the Americans and overcome their Cold War prejudices. His foreign minister, Eduard Shevardnadze, a former party secretary in Georgia, put this at the top of the perestroika agenda. Gorbachev had had partial success with Ronald Reagan at the Geneva summit in 1985 and then at Reykjavik. Finally, in a startling volte-face, that old American Cold Warrior, famous for labelling the Soviet Union 'the evil Empire', had become Gorbachev's friend and a supporter of mutually agreed arms reductions. While Gorbachev was already a hero in the West,

Gorbachev and US president Ronald Reagan in Geneva, 19 November 1985

this made Reagan a hero in the Soviet Union: when he and his wife Nancy visited in 1988, they were both greeted like rockstars.

In Britain, Margaret Thatcher, scarcely a friend of socialists, declared that she liked Gorbachev and they could do business together. Gorbachev had great success with European leaders too, including France's François Mitterrand and Germany's Helmut Kohl. Gorbachev's vision, and his way of overcoming the bipolarity of the Cold War, was to see Europe as 'our common home', and he seemed on the way to achieving this.

Eastern Europe was, on the face of it, a likely sticking point in any move towards European unity. If Eastern European countries, along with the Soviet Union, were to be encouraged to follow a path of democratic reform, there was a high probability some of them would decide to get rid of their unpopular communist regimes. Did the Brezhnev doctrine still hold? Gorbachev never showed much interest in Eastern Europe, and apparently personally despised long-time communist leaders such as East Germany's Erich Honecker and Romania's Nicolae Ceaușescu. It appears that quite early on, Gorbachev privately told the Eastern European leaders that they should look to their own legitimacy at home and not rely on Moscow in case of trouble. To Moscow, the economic advantages of Eastern Europe no doubt also seemed less now that the Soviet Union was providing these countries with oil and gas at below-market prices.

The upshot, to the world's astonishment, was that the Berlin Wall came tumbling down in 1989, Honecker's government of East Germany fell, and within a short time Germany was reunified in what was in effect a West German takeover of East Germany. Elections in Poland, Hungary and

Czechoslovakia resulted in the installation of non-communist governments; in Romania, Ceauşescu was overthrown and, by popular demand, executed. All this happened without any sign of Soviet displeasure – rather, the contrary. Gorbachev thought that he had secured verbal assurances from German foreign minister Kohl and US secretary of state James Baker that US-led NATO would not expand into Eastern Europe in the wake of the unravelling of the Soviet-led Warsaw Pact, not even into a newly unified Germany. Perhaps he had, but Gorbachev should have remembered never to trust the capitalists – and, as a lawyer, he should have known that you get your assurances in writing. By October 1990, the former German Democratic Republic was absorbed into the Federal Republic of Germany and became, ipso facto, a part of NATO.

END GAME

Gorbachev's European travels had introduced him to Scandinavian social democracy, which appealed to him. He told the party Central Committee in February 1990 that 'Our ideal is a humane, democratic socialism', adding that 'We remain committed to the choice made in October 1917'. But 'humane, democratic socialism' was *not* the choice made in October 1917. The contradictions between Gorbachev's two commitments meant that few people shared both of them, and an ever-increasing number neither. There were partisans of the Soviet system as it had evolved by Brezhnev's time, but that was about as far from the spirit of October 1917 as it was from Scandinavian social democracy. There were also opponents of the Soviet system, but not many of them were social democrats.

In the West, many people were uplifted by Gorbachev's moral political message, but it played differently in the Soviet Union. Soviet citizens were bewildered, and the legacy of Chernobyl and its contamination of large areas in Ukraine and Belorussia lent an apocalyptic tone to the popular conversation. Western anthropologists doing field work in Russia during perestroika reported an almost Dostoevskian preoccupation with suffering and the Russian soul (*dusha* – a concept disapproved of throughout the Soviet period). There was a sense of powerlessness: 'forces' were pushing the Soviet Union, who knew where or why. There was also a sense of absurdity that embraced the present and the past revolutionary dreams for which so much had been sacrificed. 'The way we live is not normal,' people kept saying. 'If only we could be a normal country.' But what normality meant, nobody seemed to know.

Chernobyl's damaged Reactor No. 4, covered with protective sarcophagus, is now in the custody of Ukraine.

Glasnost about the Soviet past on TV was too much for many viewers, who were shocked and depressed by what they learned about Gulag and other Soviet atrocities. They were upset, too, by the defection of Eastern Europe, expressing both a sense of injustice ('After all we did for them!') and a wistful bemusement ('We thought they liked us'). The new permissiveness that went with glasnost alienated many of the older generation while exciting the young: it was not morally uplifting social democratic tomes that appeared on street bookstalls, but pornography, astrology, beauty and sex handbooks, books about ESP and dark forces, anti-Semitic tracts and devotional texts, incongruously heaped together.

Though Yeltsin's career before 1985 had not suggested that he had anything in common with either Russian nationalists or liberal intellectuals, his success in becoming a focal point for both during perestroika was extraordinary. Moscow became a hive of radical activity of all kinds, and the Moscow-based Soviet media acted as a megaphone. At the same time, a somewhat sleazy and makeshift private sector blossomed, with kiosks mushrooming all over the city. There was already a 'post-Soviet' feeling in the Soviet capital during those years, with metro stations shedding the names of past Soviet leaders like Zhdanov and Kalinin and the city's major streets resuming their pre-revolutionary names (Gorky Street back to Tverskaya; Dzerzhinsky Square back to Lubyanka) at the end of 1990. Leningrad had gone even further, with a referendum narrowly won to change the name of the city back to the pre-Soviet St Petersburg.

If it had been a 'pre-crisis' situation for the Soviet economy in 1987, as Gorbachev had said, by 1990–1991 it had become a

full-blown crisis, largely as a result of Gorbachev's own policies. The high popularity ratings of Gorbachev's first years in
power dropped down to 20 per cent by 1990 and were below
zero in 1991. The growth rate of the Soviet economy had also
gone into negative territory. Oil prices spiked in November
1990, only to drop down again into the US$40 range by the
middle of the next year. But in any case Soviet oil production
was down 9 per cent on the previous year in 1991, the third
year running of decline, and there were fears that the Soviet
Union might actually have to start importing oil if the trend
continued. What had been a small budget deficit at the beginning of the 1980s had ballooned close to 58 billion roubles by
the end of 1990 (that was the official figure; US economists put
it much higher). Gold reserves plummeted; domestic prices
rose. There was rampant inflation, supply problems developed
in the towns and the incidence of street crime shot up.

Meanwhile, the ambiguous but unsettling word 'sovereignty' was to be heard in the land. It started in the Baltics,
with demands for and then declarations of sovereignty from
the popular front governments installed by the republican
elections; and by the end of 1990 had spread to virtually all the
republics, including those of Central Asia, where the declarations were made not by popular fronts opposed to the Soviet
establishment but by the local (and indigenous) Soviet estab-
lishments themselves. The republics actually possessed limited 'sovereignty' or 'sovereign rights' according to the 1936 and
1977 Soviet Constitutions, but now they wanted more. What
sovereignty meant at this point was a sharp reduction of Moscow's powers and transfer of control over resources (including

taxation) to the republics. The trend was, of course, a very alarming one for Moscow, given the possibility that, particularly in the Baltics, claims of sovereignty would morph into declarations of independence and separation from the Union. But even more disconcerting was that the Russian Republic, under Yeltsin's leadership, was one of the earliest (in June 1990) to assert the sovereignty of its territory and resources – and it soon became evident that 'resources' included taxation. The Russian Republic was the core of the Soviet Union, with 77 per cent of Soviet territory, 51 per cent of the Soviet population as of 1989, and about three-fifths of Soviet net material product. If Russia (not to mention the smaller republics) decided to keep all the taxation revenues collected there, how was the Soviet government to govern?

Historically, the Russian Republic had lacked some of the republic-specific institutions – including a Russian Communist party, KGB and Academy of Sciences – possessed by other Soviet republics. This was originally to discourage Russian nationalism, and to some extent it seemed to have worked: according to late Soviet opinion polls, Russians were more likely to think of themselves as 'Soviet' by nationality than any other ethnic group. But in administrative practice, with Moscow the capital of both the Soviet Union and the RSFSR, it often simply meant that the distinction between jurisdictions was blurred. Before perestroika, nobody had ever thought of trying to use the Russian Republic as a power base in a leadership fight. That is, until Yeltsin came along.

In the republican elections of 1990, Yeltsin was elected chairman of the Russian Supreme Soviet, which was his base until, in June 1991, he was elected by popular vote to a new position, the creation of which he was largely responsible for: the presidency of the Russian Republic. As recently as March 1987, a Russian nationalist deputy had sarcastically suggested that a Russian departure from the Union might be the solution to a problem, and his witticism had the congress laughing. But by 1990, it was no longer a joke. Russia had stopped passing on the taxes it collected to the Soviet government. Gorbachev's Soviet Union and Yeltsin's Russian Republic were precariously entangled in a new, unanticipated version of 'dual power'.

Gorbachev and Yeltsin were not the only Soviet leaders to reposition themselves as president of the jurisdictions in which they had previously been the top officials of the Communist Party. Most of the republican first secretaries did the same, so that by the autumn of 1991, the Soviet Union consisted of a number of republics headed by presidents, with a super-president, the Soviet one, putatively above them.

At first, separatism was not high on most of the republics' political agendas. The presence of twenty-five million Russians in other republics was a stumbling block, and locally the most acute form of the 'national' question was sometimes conflict between the titular nationality and other ethnic groups, as in the bloody conflict over Nagorno-Karabakh, an Armenian autonomous region within Azerbaijan. The Russian Republic, too, had its autonomous regions and republics that were starting to make assertions of sovereignty: Kazan, a historically Russian city on the Volga with a (bare) Tatar majority, declared itself the capital of Tataria, while in Chechnya (with many Chechens relatively recently returned, still angry, from exile) a national congress first called for a sovereign Chechen republic in November 1990.

Popular attitudes and elite intentions in the non-Russian republics were highly volatile. A poll conducted by a popular magazine in 1989 registered strong majority support for remaining in the Union throughout the country. But in fact the three Baltic states, never fully reconciled to their incorporation into the Soviet Union, were moving ever closer to the exit, while Moldavia, also a late acquisition, and Georgia, headed by a former dissident (Zviad Gamsakhurdia), showed similar tendencies. In Central Asia, established local leaders with strong indigenous roots were under no popular pressure to separate, but most of them were unenthusiastic about radical perestroika and privatisation, and hence increasingly suspicious of Moscow in this regard. Within the republics, many people became convinced that they were historical victims of Russian (Soviet) imperial exploitation. In the Russian Republic, of course, they thought the opposite.

A Union-wide referendum on the preservation of the USSR conducted in March 1991 still came out with a big majority in favour of a 'renewed federation of equal sovereign republics' (77 per cent voted 'yes', including 70 per cent in Ukraine). But the ambiguity of the formulation – implying that the republics should remain together, but on a different basis – was underlined by the fact that when asked whether they wanted to be part of a sovereign Ukraine within a putative Commonwealth of Sovereign States, 80 per cent of Ukrainian voters answered 'yes' to that as well. 'Union-wide', moreover, was already a reduced concept, as the six republics closest to departure from the Union – the Baltic states, Georgia, Moldova and Armenia – declined to participate in the referendum. The rump Union of nine republics sent their leaders (including Yeltsin for Russia, Nazarbayev for Kazakhstan and Leonid Kravchuk for Ukraine) to discuss the situation with Gorbachev in April, and this meeting produced an agreement to prepare a treaty establishing a 'Union of Soviet Sovereign Republics' ('socialist' was now dropped), headed by a president and with a common foreign and military policy. Under pressure from Yeltsin during subsequent drafting, the 'Union' became ever more like a confederacy, and its president progressively lost executive functions; meanwhile, Russian, Ukrainian and other republican governments continued a quiet behind-the-scenes usurpation of Soviet functions in their territories. But in any case, the treaty was never to be implemented. A coup intervened.

Gorbachev's two power bases were the Communist Party and the presidency, but the party's reputation and morale were sinking fast and the presidency was a pulpit with no supporting edifice of administrators and mobilisers. Despite continuing strong international support, Gorbachev was floundering: as had happened to the Tsar and Imperial Russia in 1916–1917, his legitimacy and that of the Soviet regime was slipping away. Any rational observer might well have expected a coup against him from left or right – most likely the right, à la General Kornilov in 1917. The coup came in mid-August, but it was ludicrously inept, a real Keystone Cops effort. Gorbachev and his family were on vacation in Foros in Crimea when a group headed by his deputy president, Gennady

Boris Yeltsin's speech from on top of a tank during the coup, 19 August 1991 (the tank operator buries his head in his hands)

Yanayev, defence minister Dmitry Yazov, and KGB head Vladimir Kryuchkov flew down to ask him to proclaim a national emergency. When he refused, they flew back to Moscow and proclaimed the emergency themselves, with Yanayev as acting president during Gorbachev's alleged illness. The Gorbachevs, meanwhile, were left for several days incommunicado and under house arrest at their dacha in Foros.

The attempted coup was very much a Moscow enterprise, with no serious attempt to get republican leaders onside. Azerbaijan's leader was the only one to issue a statement supporting the coup; the majority prudently waited to see what would happen. Perhaps, like Kornilov before them, the Moscow plotters thought they were doing Gorbachev a favour by taking the initiative to save the country from disintegration. But their performance announcing this on television was woeful, and tens of thousands came out in protest on the streets of Moscow. Army troops and tanks were brought into the centre of the city, but without orders or inclination to shoot. Yeltsin, remaining at liberty through the incompetence of the plotters, became the hero of the hour: photographs of him on top of a tank went round the world. The plotters lost their nerve, and Gorbachev was released and returned to Moscow. But his political stature, and the prospects for survival of the Soviet Union, had received a fatal blow.

In the wake of the coup, Yeltsin, as head of the Russian Republic, suspended the activities of the Communist Party in its territories. Ukraine, after a slow start, had had an upsurge of nationalist support, with a referendum on 1 December

Gorbachev and family returning from Foros, 22 August 1991

1991 producing a 90 per cent vote in favour of independence with an 84 per cent turnout (which meant that not only had the majority of the republic's Ukrainians voted for it, but the majority of its Russians had too).

Early in August, US president George H.W. Bush had supported Gorbachev and the preservation of the Union, warning against 'suicidal nationalism' in a speech – disrespectfully nicknamed 'Chicken Kiev' by critics at home – in the Ukrainian capital. But by November Bush was backing off under intense pressure from congress and the Ukrainian lobby. Ukraine's imminent defection, and the United States' likely acquiescence in it, were important nails in the Soviet coffin.

It was Yeltsin who was nevertheless the main executor of the Soviet Union's demise. Princess Diana famously said of her marriage that it was a bit crowded with three people in it. The same was true of two presidents in Moscow. Of the pair, Gorbachev, not being popularly elected, found himself in the weaker position. Had he resigned after the coup, opening the way for Yeltsin to succeed him in the senior office of Soviet president, the Soviet Union might not have disintegrated so completely as it did subsequently, because Yeltsin would then have had an interest in its survival, albeit in revised form, rather than its collapse. But it was not until 25 December 1991 that Gorbachev resigned the Soviet presidency – and by that time, on Yeltsin's initiative, the heads of the Russian, Ukrainian and Belorussian republics had met secretly and agreed on an a much-diminished successor to the Soviet Union, a Commonwealth of Independent States, with a unified military but no central president or parliament, which

Dzerzhinsky's statue, toppled on 23 August 1991, now stands in the Park of Fallen Monuments in Moscow. Since 2006, an exact copy stands in Belarus's capital, Minsk.

was ratified by the three republics a few days later. When US secretary of state Baker came to Moscow a week later, he was received in the Kremlin by Russian president Yeltsin, with new Soviet defence minister Marshal Evgeny Shaposhnikov in tow. Gorbachev's resignation was a recognition of an already existing situation – that the nation of which he was president no longer existed.

Multiple hands were working behind the scenes to secure, hide or appropriate assets of the Soviet government and the Soviet Communist Party (dissolved after the coup) located in Moscow, but it was Yeltsin, on behalf of the Russian Republic, who got the lion's share. The republican leaders followed suit with regard to the assets of the states and Communist parties in their territories. The Russian Republic now became the successor state to the Soviet Union, the Russian tricolour replacing the Soviet flag above the Kremlin. The other republics – some enthusiastically, others because they had no alternative – declared themselves to be sovereign independent states. The Soviet Union, just a decade earlier an apparently stable superpower with a strong military and police, and a ruling party that had recently had almost twenty million members, had self-destructed without a shot being fired in its defence.

POST-SOVIET RE-INVENTION

After the 1917 Revolution, Russians had had to re-invent themselves to suit the new world, discovering proletarian ancestors and off-loading aristocrats from the family tree. The same was true after 1991, only in reverse. Thus in Soviet times the poet Demian Bednyi presented himself as coming from the poor peasantry, but in the 1990s his grandson supported claims to aristocratic lineage by citing the old (once discreditable) rumour that Demian was the illegitimate son of a Tsarist Grand Duke. Nobody knew how to address groups of unknown people: was 'comrades' still acceptable, or should it be 'citizens' or even 'ladies and gentlemen'? So many new terms were imported from English that new dictionaries of post-Soviet speech were needed. How could one navigate the new world without words like *menedzhery* (managers) and *brokery* (brokers)? Everyone wanted to become a *biznesmen* (businessman), but whether the female form was *biznes-ledi* or *biznesmenka* was unclear. For capitalist entrepreneurial activities; *pablik-rileishnz* (public relations), *konsalting* (consulting) and *rieltory* (real estate agents) were essential, and the media now had to worry about *reitingi* (ratings). Shopping was a pastime of discerning consumers that had nothing to do with the old Soviet hunter-gatherer approach to acquiring goods. The guru and *ektrasens* (practitioner of ESP) became TV familiars, and for those interested in *ufologiia* (the study of unidentified flying objects), a *kontakter* (f. *kontaktërsha*) was desirable to 'enter into contact with non-Earth civilisations.' Even sex was different under capitalism: in a Foucauldian move, it became a discourse of *seks* that could only be conducted through Western neologisms (*gei*, *biseksualy*).

Conclusion

Huge amounts of blood were shed to make and maintain the Soviet Union. Some of it was the blood of idealists, some of thugs and careerists, but most of it was the blood of ordinary people whose main concern was survival. The country shut itself off from the rest of the world for decades, 'building socialism', a substantial part of which consisted of strengthening and modernising the state. That state committed major crimes against its people: the Great Purges, kulak and national deportations, and the creation and expansion of Gulag. Then came the long-feared external bloodletting, World War II. After the war, in the wake of tens of millions of human losses and tremendous destruction, and with the borders closed again, things gradually settled down. Almost fifty years passed without major bloodshed or upheavals.

Out of all this turmoil came the Brezhnevian Soviet Union with which our story started. This was a welfare state, still comparatively poor, but fairly egalitarian. Everyone could get an education and a job, although the big opportunities of the prewar years for upward (or downward) mobility had gone. High culture had been brought to the masses, although this irked some of its creators, as did their protection from 'decadent' trends of the West. Men drank heavily without social censure; women, still forced to use abortion as a family-planning tool, bore the double burden of work and home duties. Multiculturalism (to use an anachronistic term) was a basic societal commitment; public expressions of ethnic prejudice were taboo. Corruption flourished at the interstices of the state-owned economy with its creaky system of centralised planning. The smokestack industry, whose construction was the pride of the 1930s, had done great damage to the environment, as the Chernobyl disaster underlined. The regime's avowed commitment to international peace went with a lot of spending on the military. Borders were now slightly ajar, but not enough for the educated middle class. The security services had given up terror; surveillance and punishment were no longer inflicted randomly but instead focused on individuals who had decided to embrace the role of dissidents – a relatively small number, but with the foreign 'Voices' such as Radio Liberty serving as an echo chamber. Cultivation of the private sphere was a watchword, but the predictable, humdrum tenor of Soviet life, with the smug didacticism of Soviet propaganda as its over-familiar backdrop, appealed more to the old than the young.

Brezhnev called this 'socialism', and it certainly met many of the formal criteria – state ownership, welfare protection, emancipation of women and tolerance of ethnic diversity. It had the disadvantage of requiring the Soviet Union to be semi-isolated from the world, and it was short on democracy, in the sense of popular ability to elect and remove leaders or choose among competing political parties. But lack of democracy was not a great concern for most of its citizens; the main grievances were more material. 'Socialism' was meant to deliver abundance, but the Soviet standard of living was below that of the developed West, and after the 1960s it no longer looked as if that gap would be bridged any time soon. If this was indeed socialism, it seemed that many Soviet citizens wanted something more.

The moment the Soviet Union was gone, everyone started calling it an 'empire'. That term had not been used in the Soviet Union, since in Soviet terms it was only capitalists who had empires, and in the West it had mainly been used in the context of an 'evil empire'. But in the early 1990s the word became ubiquitous, and for understandable reasons: a multinational state that suddenly loses its peripheries must surely be an empire, and once it was seen as an empire, its collapse was easy to explain in terms of its colonies (the non-Russian Soviet republics) liberating themselves from exploitation by the imperial centre (Moscow and the Russians). This was plausible, but only partly accurate.

In the first place, the assumption that Moscow was profiting economically from its 'colonies' is doubtful. People in the non-Russian republics came to see it that way during perestroika. On the other hand, people in Russia saw it as the opposite, with the economic advantage on the side of the republics, and Western economists, while generally avoiding the topic as a can of worms too complicated to unravel, are inclined to agree with the Russians. In the second place, the 'liberation' model suggests that the colonial populations rose up against their oppressors and drove them out. With a bit of a stretch, that could fit what happened in the Baltic republics (which the Soviet Union could afford to lose), but it scarcely

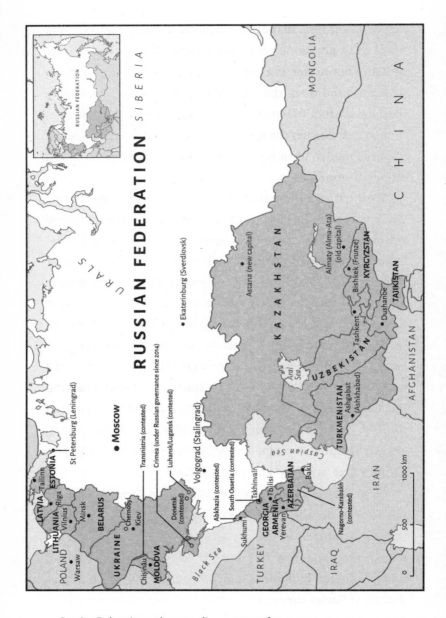

Russian Federation and surrounding states as of 2014

applies to the rest. In the majority of cases, republican leaders made their decisions *not* as the result of irresistible popular pressure but rather as a consequence of the Union's collapse, which offered them the remarkable opportunity to become national leaders, essentially cost-free. In doing so, moreover, they were following the lead of Russia, which, if we follow the imperial model, must be seen as liberating itself from its own 'imperial' domination.

Western commentators predicted a democratic post-Soviet future for Russia (and, hopefully, for the rest of the new states as well), as its economy inevitably expanded under the benign influence of the market. But Russians with a sense of history braced themselves for a time of troubles. No more than a fifth of respondents to opinion polls in the 1990s thought that Russia would benefit from 'democracy' in its Western forms, and observation of post-Soviet political practice generated widespread negative reactions to the word itself, along with 'freedom' and 'elections'. In response to a 1999 poll asking Russians which of thirteen variables were most important to them, 'democracy' came in second last, less popular than any of the options except 'freedom of entrepreneurship'. Top choices were 'stability' and 'social welfare'.

Shok was the ubiquitous new word of the tumultuous first post-Soviet decade under President Yeltsin. 'Shock therapy' was the approach of the privatisation policy Yeltsin introduced, formulated with advice from Western economists and conducted by Egor Gaidar (son of a famous children's author of Soviet times). Considering that almost everything had previously belonged to the state, privatisation was a huge undertaking with no precedents to provide guidelines. Russians called the result 'wild capitalism', a process whereby everyone grabbed whatever assets they could – those with higher positions and better connections in the old state and party apparatus being able to seize more – and then stood guard over them. Even liberal academics from the Higher Party School (Yury Afanasiev's institute) were galvanised to march across town and commandeer a more desirable campus. Guns, whose private ownership had not been allowed in the Soviet Union, proliferated, as did security guards in camouflage fatigues with their shirts open to display gold chains. Everyone was looking for protection (a 'roof'), and it was often hard to tell whether the groups that provided it were police, criminal groups or a mixture of both.

Apartments, previously rented at low cost from the state, were privatised, with renters able to buy them at advantageous rates. The problem with this was that criminals might then come demanding extortionate payments and, in the event of non-payment, turn residents out onto the streets. Those who remained bought steel doors for their apartments, but that didn't keep them safe on the stairwells or in the lifts, so apartment blocks started installing gates and Western-style buzzers at their entrances. Urban dwellers who also had a dacha in the countryside often retreated to it, renting out the city apartment to make ends meet. 'Cultivating one's garden' was not just a metaphor but a near-universal pursuit of the 1990s, as price controls on basic commodities were lifted and prices soared.

Inflation and non-payment of salaries reduced pensioners and many white-collar workers to penury. Old women stood

outside metro stations, speechlessly holding out a few rad-
ishes or a pair of woollen gloves in the hope a hurrying com-
muter might buy them. Beggars and homeless people were
suddenly part of the urban landscape. Working people with
a solid workplace such as a factory or office clung to it, even
when they stopped being paid, both for the camaraderie and
for any provisions that might show up for internal distribution. Peasants on the collective farms looked hopefully at the
kolkhoz chairman to keep things running. Intellectuals were
particularly hard hit, not just by poverty (as their salaries shriv-
elled to nearly nothing) but by the collapse of the staple institutions of their lives, such as the 'thick' journals. The high value
they – and the Soviet state – had placed on education and high
culture seemed ridiculous to their grandchildren, who were
rapidly learning American and looking for a way to make a
fast buck. With sixty thousand suicides in 2002, Russia had
the highest per capita rate in the world. Male life expectancy
dropped sharply from just under sixty-four at the beginning
of the 1990s to fifty-eight a decade later, and didn't start rising
again until 2005. Russia's women, long renowned for their
resilience in the face of hardship, showed it again by losing
only two and a half years' life expectancy over the same period.
Some, eager to unemancipate, embraced the housewife's role.

Some Russians did well, mainly on the basis of quick
reactions when the moment to appropriate a former state
asset arrived. 'New Russians' was the term for the nouveaux
riches, and 'oligarchs' was the term for the small group of
the extremely rich, including Boris Berezovsky and Mikhail
Khodorkovsky, on whose approval Yeltsin's regime was

thought to depend. Berezovsky, a mathematician and engineer who in late Soviet times had been a department head in an institute of the Academy of Sciences, made his fortune by acquiring Russia's main TV channel; Khodorkovsky, a Komsomol official who started his business career by setting up a private cafe under perestroika, went into private banking and managed to acquire Yukos Oil from the state at a bargain price in the mid-1990s. Given the way these fortunes were amassed, there was always a taint of illegality attached. Russia's new 'capitalism', while partly based on Western models, was also a direct successor to the old Soviet 'second economy', functioning on the basis of personal ties rather than contracts in a grey area of legality.

Russia's new rich were notable for their extremely conspicuous consumption, including dachas that grew into baroque castles, to the wonder of neighbouring village dwellers. They also spent a lot of time in the West, sending their sons to elite schools in Britain and Switzerland, and parking much of their newly gained wealth abroad. Unrestricted Western travel for those who could afford it was one of the great boons of the post-Soviet period for Russians; it turned out that of all the restrictions imposed by the Soviet system, this one had been particularly irksome. Now, for the first time in seventy years, it was possible for Russians to leave their country (other than as tourists) without considering themselves émigrés. High-profile intellectuals and artists, as well as businessmen, could now establish residences on both sides of the border. Young women responding to the lure of open borders could now find themselves in Europe, working as prostitutes.

The new Russia had a free press, varied in political complexion and hot on the track of current scandals, real and imagined, as well as historical ones. But the most daring journalists lived a risky life, and journalistic assassinations – as well as assassinations of businessmen by their rivals – became comparatively common. The intelligentsia was flattened by the collapse of perestroika (for which it, along with Gorbachev, was blamed by much of the population), and its members, suffering from loss of status and the discrediting of their claims to moral leadership, had difficulty finding their footing in the new Russia. Political parties came into existence; a revived Russian Communist Party gained the most traction in the 1990s, but there were also liberal and nationalist parties around and, at street level, some quasi-Nazi bullyboys. The parties contested elections to the new parliament, named a Duma as in tsarist times. The Duma became the site of many lively discussions and some extraordinary legislation (one law 'restored' the Soviet Union), but as the president was not obliged to approve its legislation, it didn't matter too much. President Yeltsin himself had not formed a party. He was a drinker with a heart problem, and both his health and his behaviour became increasingly erratic.

While the KGB survived the change of regime under a new name (Federal Security Service, or FSB) and kept control of its archives, the Soviet Communist Party lost its archives, along with the rest of its property, to the new Russian Federation, which threw them open. They were mined as evidence for a trial of the Soviet Communist Party's legality in Russia's Constitutional Court in 1992, sparked by a suit brought by former

Communists claiming that Yeltsin's dissolution of the Communist Party the previous year had been unconstitutional. This provoked a countersuit asserting that what had been unconstitutional was the whole period of Communist Party rule since 1917. The trial was to be a boon to historians, since it declassified a mass of previously secret documents, but *The Washington Post*'s correspondent in Moscow, dutifully attending the hearings, was surprised to find that nobody else seemed to care.

An early popular reaction to the collapse of the Soviet Union was to pretend that the seventy-four years separating the new Russian Federation from its pre-revolutionary precursor had never existed. That tsarist past was something that people were eager to reclaim in these years. The old imperial two-headed eagle returned as a state symbol. Russians

Lenin statues, on the left, in their new home in Moscow's Park of Fallen Monuments

re-embraced a half-remembered Orthodoxy and rediscovered noble ancestors, just as they had discovered proletarian ones at the beginning of the Soviet period. Restaurants opened with kitschy pseudo-imperial decor. Psychics and sorcerers became wildly popular, and an astrologer was one of the most beloved figures on television. Revolution Day on 7 November remained a public holiday, but under the optimistic new name of 'Day of Reconciliation and Accord'. So many monuments of Soviet leaders came down that Moscow had to establish a special park to put them in. But the city also acquired a new Cathedral of Christ the Saviour, erected not far from the Kremlin in the place where its predecessor, blown up by the Soviets in 1931, had once stood.

The question of whether a new 'Soviet' identity and nationality were emerging, as claimed in the 1977 Constitution, had been a topic of controversy in late Soviet times, but now it could be confidently answered in the affirmative. *Sovok* (literally, dustpan) was the new pejorative term for 'Soviet man' (and woman), and such benighted people were regularly mocked in the press. An *Interpretative Dictionary of the Language of Sovdepia* (the Soviet Union) was published as a guide (or memorial) to Soviet linguistic usage. There were also much needed new dictionaries of foreign words and recent changes in spoken and written Russian. The language of the mass media was suddenly and drastically Westernised, with huge numbers of invented words that sounded as bizarre in Russian as Soviet acronyms had once done. A popular novel of the 1990s, Viktor Pelevin's *Homo Zapiens* was a black comedy set in the new world of advertising and television, in which *imidzh* (image) and *pi-ar* (PR or public relations) were everything and core identities had disappeared.

It was not just individuals who were in the process of self-reinvention. The same was true, even more dramatically, of the new nation states – now, as one commentator observed, abruptly thrust into the business of statehood before they had achieved nationhood. Many of them were led by the former first party secretaries of their republics, who had negotiated the transition to president shortly before the collapse and held onto the job. Nursultan Nazarbayev, who would resign as president of the new independent Kazakhstan in 2019 at the age of seventy-eight, was one of them, as were the presidents of Azerbaijan, Uzbekistan and Turkmenistan, where Saparmurat Niyazov went one better than the rest by making himself 'president for life'. Georgia, to be sure, was headed by a former dissident and Shakespeare scholar, Zviad Gamsakhurdia, until his replacement by Gorbachev's former foreign minister, Eduard Shevardnadze, who was in turn replaced by a free-market enthusiast, Mikheil Saakashvili, whose status as a perestroika-era graduate of a Ukrainian university could, in earlier times, have been cited as an example of Soviet 'friendship of peoples'. Other improvised leadership styles in the region included that of a former Komsomol activist in the North Caucasus, captured by Georgi Derluguian (in *Bourdieu's Secret Admirer in the Caucasus*) in the act of self-reinvention as an Islamic leader of a nationalist rebellion against the new hegemon, independent Georgia.

If the federal Soviet Union could fall apart into a bunch of separate independent national states, why not the Russian Republic? Here the potential seceders included Tatarstan (formerly the Tartar autonomous republic, or Tartaria) and Chechnya. But Yeltsin, and Vladimir Putin after him, drew a line in the sand on this one. In the case of Chechnya, that meant a war – one of many post-Soviet nationality-based conflicts, including the Nagorno-Karabakh conflict, involving Armenia and Azerbaijan – that was to be a running sore for years. Tatarstan took a different tack, signing a treaty with Russia giving Tatars 'equal sovereignty' (but not independent sovereignty) and a share in the republic's oil revenues, and being rewarded by Putin with a new metro system for Kazan.

Internationally, post-Soviet Russia was the beneficiary of a lot of American tutelage and private investment, and managed to hang on to the Soviet seat on the United Nations Security

Before and after: Saparmurat Niyazov as first secretary of the Communist Party of Soviet Turkmenistan and as president of (independent post-Soviet) Turkmenistan

Council. But its status in the world was greatly reduced, and it had to accept the eastward expansion of NATO that Gorbachev thought the West had promised *not* to allow. Poland, the Czech Republic and Hungary were admitted to NATO in 1999, while Slovakia, Slovenia, Bulgaria, Romania and the three Baltic republics followed in 2004. Still worse, from the Russian standpoint, Ukraine and Georgia, although not yet admitted to NATO, were recognised as being in the waiting line. It was questionable whether Russia was even a global power anymore, let alone a superpower. Of course it was still a regional power, but its region consisted primarily of former Soviet republics and former Soviet bloc nations. Having encouraged the republics to leave the Union in 1991, Yeltsin and his foreign minister, Andrei Kozyrev, quickly changed their approach and let it be known that they saw the Russian Republic as a natural magnet around which other neighbouring states were likely to regather in some form or other. But the response was lukewarm: letting the genie of separatism out of the bottle was a lot easier than putting it back in. In Russia, meanwhile, opinion polls suggested that 71 per cent thought the breakup of the Soviet Union had been a mistake.

Yeltsin stayed at the helm for most of the 1990s, but a financial crisis in 1998 brought the country to the brink of bankruptcy, with the Russian Central Bank defaulting on its debt and devaluing the rouble. Looking around for a successor as his health deteriorated, Yeltsin hit on a little-known ex-KGB man named Vladimir Putin, a judo aficionado with a low-key manner, who had been working in the Kremlin administration for the past few years. Yeltsin appointed Putin as his prime minister in 1999, thus allowing him to become acting president when Yeltsin resigned a few months later. In the 2000 presidential elections, to the surprise of many, but helped by Russian military successes in Chechnya, Putin won 53 per cent of the popular vote in the first round.

Putin once described himself, not without a tinge of irony, as 'an absolutely successful product of the patriotic education of a Soviet man'. Born at the height of postwar privation to working-class parents in Leningrad, he had trained as a lawyer and then joined the KGB out of conviction and romanticism (heroic spy stories were popular in the Soviet Union in his youth). For the last ten years of his not particularly distinguished Soviet career, he served as a Soviet agent in East Germany, observing its dramatic collapse in 1989 before returning to the gathering chaos of the Soviet Union. He never formally left the Communist Party, simply putting his party card away in a drawer when it became irrelevant. Back in Russia, he worked for Leningrad leader Anatoly Sobchak before moving to Moscow in 1996. Putin was not only a product of Lenin's city – Leningrad – but even had a tenuous family connection with Lenin via his grandfather, who had worked as a cook for Lenin's widow back in the 1920s. Had it still been Soviet times, someone would surely have pointed out that a cook's grandson at the head of the government was a fulfilment of Lenin's prediction in *State and Revolution*.

Putin's early performance as a leader was unexpectedly impressive. Positioning himself as a (moderate) Russian nationalist and Orthodox believer, but with a respect for the Soviet past, he set out to rein in the oligarchs, stop the disintegration of Russia (as in the case of Chechnya), correct the excesses of 'wild capitalism' and reassert a degree of state control over the financial system and key industries such as gas. His efforts were aided by rising international oil prices, which in 2008 stood at US$137 a barrel before dropping again from 2014. He offered stability and the hope of restoring some of Russia's lost international status, and was repaid by high to very high approval ratings (attested by independent as well as state opinion polls). As part of his campaign against the Yeltsin-era oligarchs, Boris Berezovsky was forced into emigration (he would die in London in mysterious circumstances in 2013), while Mikhail Khodorkovsky was charged with financial crimes in 2003 and served a prison term before leaving the country.

In a drawn-out pull-and-push conflict, Putin gradually increased presidential power to dismiss provincial governors at odds with Moscow. Politically, he had the support of a new national party, United Russia, that ran candidates in elections for the Duma and which all provincial governors were expected to join (it was more a mechanism for delivering votes and choosing candidates for federal office, like Richard Daley's famous 'party machine' in Chicago, than a conventional party, and Putin, like Mayor Daley, operated without a Politburo). Relying partly on *siloviki* – people, such as Putin himself, who came out of the Soviet military and security police – his administration proved increasingly intolerant of political challenge (despite the maintenance of an electoral framework) and manipulated the system to stay in power when his constitutional term ran out in 2008. As of 2021, at the age of sixty-eight, he was in his fourth term as Russia's president.

After initial overtures, Putin seemed to have given up on restoring good relations with the West, and perhaps even started to enjoy thumbing his nose at Western public opinion. The 'colour' revolutions of 2003–2005 in Georgia, Ukraine and Kyrgyzstan played an important part in this estrangement, since the Russian leaders were convinced that NATO and the United States had been behind them, aiming to destabilise governments sympathetic to Russia, and might try the same techniques on Russia itself. Putin's KGB past seemed to resurface with 'dirty tricks' evidently emanating from his administration, such as the poisoning in England of former Russian intelligence agents Alexander Litvinenko in 2006 and Sergei Skripal in 2018. In 2014, Russia reclaimed Crimea, presented to Soviet Ukraine in 1954 by Khrushchev in an expansive gesture. Crimea, important to Russia as the seat of the Black Sea Fleet, was predominantly Russian-speaking, with about two-thirds of its population identifying as ethnic Russians, the rest being mainly Ukrainians and Crimean Tatars (who had returned after the collapse of the Soviet Union from their enforced exile in the 1940s). Russia also more or less covertly supported and sponsored separatist movements in Ukraine's eastern Donbass and Lugansk provinces, home to about a seventh of Ukraine's population, in which ethnic Russians were almost as numerous as Ukrainians. These actions provoked outrage in the West, but were popular in Russia.

For the majority of Russians who regretted the passing of the Soviet Union, the whole Soviet period, from NEP to the beginning of perestroika, was remembered (not, of course, with perfect accuracy) as a time of public order, safety and low prices on basic goods. As the Soviet population reassessed its past leaders, Brezhnev was the big beneficiary. To many in the early 2000s, the Brezhnev era stood out as a golden age. 'Neither wars nor revolutions. Neither famine nor upheavals,' wrote an admiring Russian biographer of Brezhnev in 2002. A better life for 'the simple Soviet toiler, that is for the great majority of the people'; in short, 'the best time in the whole much-suffering twentieth century'.

Yeltsin and Gorbachev got short shrift from the public in a 2017 poll that found that 'anger, contempt' were the predominant feelings of 30 per cent of respondents towards them both, while an additional 15–13 per cent picked 'disgust, hate'. This was a markedly different attitude to Gorbachev than the admiration and sympathy prevalent in the West: for Russians, he was not the hero of democratic reform, but the man who lost the Union. The two former leaders did not, however, become 'non-persons' in the good old Soviet tradition: at ninety, Gorbachev was still formally president of the non-profit Gorbachev Foundation, while Yeltsin, who died in 2007, was honoured by a spectacular Yeltsin Museum in his native Urals.

The same 2017 poll showed that in terms of public esteem, Stalin (with 32 per cent of respondents choosing 'respect' as the best description of their attitude to him) scored higher than any leader but Putin (49 per cent), with Lenin in third place at 26 per cent. For a humiliated nation, Stalin was the historical exemplar of national pride and achievement – the builder of the nation and its industrial might, and the man who led that nation to victory in World War II. The repressive side of Stalin's legacy seemed of lesser interest to most post-Soviet Russians.

Mikhail Gorbachev in retirement in 2014 with American Sovietologist Stephen F. Cohen (seated) and his wife, Katrina vanden Heuvel. Behind them is Dmitry Muratov, editor of *Novaia Gazeta* and winner of the 2021 Nobel Peace Prize.

World War II became central to the national myth of the new Russian Federation, just as it had been to the Soviet state that preceded it, and Stalin epitomised the victory. Since 2014, Russians can be punished for presenting an unflattering picture of Soviet activities during the war, and in 2021 the lower house of the Duma passed a law punishing insults to World War II veterans by up to five years in prison. These besmirchers often come from Ukraine, rehabilitating wartime anti-Soviet nationalist partisans like the 'Benderites'. Ukraine, meanwhile, was developing its own national foundation myth, sharply at odds with the Russian one. It focused on Holodomor, the famine of the early 1930s, reinterpreted as genocide against the Ukrainian people.

Putin was one of those who admired Stalin as a nation builder. He raised a toast to Stalin's birthday at a meeting with Duma leaders in December 1999, and in 2000, one of his first acts as president was to reinstall the old Soviet national anthem as Russia's anthem – admittedly with new words, but these were written by the author of the original lyrics, Sergei Mikhalkov, an esteemed Soviet writer who in his time had won three Stalin Prizes. Putin at first had little to say about Stalin's terror, but this was a major concern of his political ally, the Orthodox Church. By 2017, in company with Patriarch Kirill, he was unveiling a monument in Moscow to victims of political repression, and the next year doing the same for Aleksandr Solzhenitsyn (the erstwhile dissident who had returned to Russia in 1994), with the comment that the Soviet 'totalitarian system had brought suffering and great hardship to millions'.

Most people who like Stalin also like Lenin – but that doesn't apply to Putin, despite his grandfather's relationship to him. In 2017, Putin passed up the opportunity to have a big celebration of the hundredth anniversary of the Russian Revolution. He had issues with Lenin over the bloodshed of the civil war and the execution of the Tsar's entire family, and even their dog, in 1918. But his real problem with Lenin was that, as a revolutionary, he was a nation destroyer, not a nation builder like Stalin. Over Stalin's objections, Putin the amateur historian recalled, Lenin insisted on inserting a clause in the original Soviet Constitution giving republics the right of secession. 'It was a time bomb, pointing at us,' Putin observed. Khrushchev also earned his ire on a similar issue, the transfer of Crimea to Ukraine in 1954, by which – Putin told the Duma on 18 March 2014 – Russia was 'not simply robbed, it was plundered'.

President Putin and Patriarch Kirill at Easter service in Moscow's Christ the Saviour Cathedral, 24 April 2015

People around the world rejoiced in the disappearance of the Soviet Union as a state where much evil was done, although a few mourned it as at least an attempt at socialism. But for many Russians, whose birth state it was, the narrative was different. Coming out of backwardness, Russia had miraculously won its twentieth-century place in the sun, first leading the world towards socialism and later becoming a superpower – and then all that was suddenly snatched away for no apparent reason, along with the respect of the world and the empire inherited from the Tsars. Adding insult to injury, the West continued, after a brief interlude in the 1990s, to treat Russia with almost the same degree of hostility as when it had been the enemy superpower in the Cold War. This amounted to xenophobia in Russian eyes. ('Before, they said they hated us because we were communists, but then we stopped being communist and they still hate us.')

With regard to future restoration, Putin's aphoristic summary was that 'anyone who feels no regret for the passing of the Soviet Union has no heart, and anyone who hopes to restore it has no brain'. But who knows what the future holds? A leader with a brain (someone like Putin?) might see a way to recover some of what was lost, even if it fell short of 'restoration'. Why should Ukraine suffer the tremendous economic losses and 'deindustrialisation' arising out of separation from Russia, Putin reflected in an interview in 2020, when 'we are the same people', and together could become a global player again? The invasion of Ukraine in February 2022, while making such an outcome extremely unlikely for the foreseeable future, showed that this was no idle musing. The ghost of the Soviet Union was not going to disappear as quickly as the Soviet Union itself had done. Still, the sense of holding History's mandate, which inspired Soviet leaders from Lenin to Gorbachev, was non-recoverable. Putin, as a good Soviet citizen schooled in Marxism–Leninism, had no doubt once believed in historical inevitability. Not anymore; not since that knockout demonstration of the irresistible power of contingency in 1989–1991. As he said in an interview in 2000:

You know there's a lot that seems impossible and incredible and then – *bang!* Look what happened to the Soviet Union. Who could have imagined that it would simply collapse?

Acknowledgements

The four dedicatees should be acknowledged first for their contribution to my understanding of Soviet history, in conversation and argument as well as through their published works. As my self-appointed mentor from my earliest days in Moscow as a graduate student on the British Exchange in the late 1960s, Igor Sats played a huge part in forming my view of the Soviet Union. Jerry Hough, to whom I was married in the years 1975–1983, taught me a great deal about Soviet politics and shared many of the experiences that inform the story told in this book. Seweryn Bialer, my colleague and interlocutor at Columbia University in the 1970s, added his distinctive perspective on Communist affairs as a former insider. Stephen F. Cohen, who when I first arrived in the United States recruited me as an ally in Sovietological conflicts and later regretted it, was at first a critic and rival, and then, with the passing of the years, a friend.

The writing of this book took me into some aspects of Soviet history that I knew largely through the primary research of others, a number of them my PhD students at the University of Chicago in the 1990s and 2000s. On Soviet nationalities, I owe a large debt to Ronald Suny, Vera Tolz-Zilitinkevic, Yuri Slezkine, Marianne Kamp, Matthew Payne, Terry Martin, Michael Westren, Andrew Sloin, Flora Roberts and Michaela Pohl, as well as the editors of *Ab Imperio*, since reading through the entire run of their post-Soviet journal was a stimulating and profitable part of my preparation for this book. On the regions and regional administration, the debt is to Yoram Gorlizki, Jonathan Bone, James Harris, Golfo Alexopoulos, Alan Barenberg and Julia Fine; on public health to Christopher Burton, Benjamin Zajicek and Michael David; on wars and their aftermaths to Joshua Sanborn, Roger Reese, Jeong-Ha Lee, Natalie Belsky and Mark Edele; and on the economy, Stephen Wheatcroft, Oscar Sibony-Sanchez, Charles Hachten, Julie Hessler, Kyung Deok Roh and Kristy Ironside.

My heartfelt thanks for help and support in locating materials go to the late June Farris and Sandra Levy, Slavic librarians at the University of Chicago; Chris Franz at East View Press; and Rena McGrogan at the University of Sydney.

Kate Fullagar, my colleague at Australian Catholic University, inadvertently prompted me to think about starting my story in 1980 through her discussion of writing history backwards.

I am enormously grateful to the four people who read the manuscript or a substantial portion of it and made detailed and very helpful comments and criticisms: Vera Tolz-Zilitinkevic, Graeme Gill, Chris Feik and Ruth Balint. The book was much improved as a result. Katja Heath did sterling service in searching out the illustrations.

The team at Black Inc. was exemplary, and I thank them all warmly: Chris Feik (who suggested the project in the first place), Kate Hatch, Kate Nash, Erin Sandiford and Julia Carlomagno.

Further Reading

This is not offered as a comprehensive bibliography but rather as a guide to works, including my own, on which I have drawn heavily in writing this book.

GENERAL

Davies, R.W., Mark Harrison and S.G. Wheatcroft, *The Economic Transformation of the Soviet Union, 1913–1945*, Cambridge University Press, Cambridge, 1994.

Fitzpatrick, Sheila, *On Stalin's Team: The Years of Living Dangerously in Soviet Politics*, Princeton University Press, Princeton, 2015.

Fitzpatrick, Sheila, *The Russian Revolution*, 4th edition, Oxford University Press, Oxford, 2017.

Gorlizki, Yoram and Oleg Khlevniuk, *Substate Dictatorships: Networks, Loyalty, and Institutional Change in the Soviet Union*, Yale University Press, New Haven, 2020.

Hanson, Philip, *The Rise and Fall of the Soviet Economy: An Economic History of the USSR, 1945–1991*, Routledge, London, 2014.

Hough, Jerry F. and Merle Fainsod, *How the Soviet Union Is Governed*, Harvard University Press, Cambridge, MA, 1982.

Lovell, Stephen, *The Shadow of War: Russia and the USSR, 1941 to the Present*, Wiley-Blackwell, Chichester, 2010.

Nove, Alec, *An Economic History of the USSR, 1917–1991*, 3rd edition, Penguin, London, 1992.

Rigby, T.H., *Communist Party Membership in the USSR, 1917–1967*, Princeton University Press, Princeton, 1968.

Siegelbaum, Lewis H. and Leslie Page Moch, *Broad Is My Native Land: Repertoires and Regimes of Migration in Russia's Twentieth Century*, Cornell University Press, Ithaca, 2014.

Simon, Gerhard, *Nationalism and Policy toward the Nationalities in the Soviet Union*, trans. Karen Forster and Oswald Forster, Westview Press, Boulder, 1991.

Slezkine, Yuri, 'The Soviet Union as a Communal Apartment', *Slavic Review*, vol. 53, no. 2, 1994, republished in Sheila Fitzpatrick (ed.), *Stalinism: New Directions*, Routledge, London and New York, 2000.

Slezkine, Yuri, *The Jewish Century*, Princeton University Press, Princeton, 2011.

Suny, Ronald Grigor, *The Soviet Experiment: Russia, the USSR, and the Successor States*, Oxford University Press, New York, 2011.

INTRODUCTION

Bialer, Seweryn, *Stalin's Successors: Leadership, Stability, and Change in the Soviet Union*, Cambridge University Press, Cambridge, 1980.

Cohen, Stephen F., Alexander Rabinowitch and Robert S. Sharlet (eds), *The Soviet Union since Stalin*, Macmillan, London, 1980.

Verdery, Katherine, *What Was Socialism, and What Comes Next?*, Princeton University Press, Princeton, 1996.

CHAPTER 1

Henderson, Robert, *The Spark That Lit the Revolution: Lenin in London and the Politics That Changed the World*, I.B. Tauris, London, 2020.

Pipes, Richard, *Russia under the Old Regime*, Penguin, Harmondsworth, 1977.

Solzhenitsyn, Alexander, *Lenin in Zurich*, trans. H.T. Willetts, Penguin, Harmondsworth, 1976.

Sukhanov, N.N. (ed.), *The Russian Revolution, 1917: Eyewitness Account*, abr. Joel Carmichael, Harper, New York, 1962.

CHAPTER 2

Cohen, Stephen F., *Bukharin and the Bolshevik Revolution: A Political Biography, 1888–1938*, Alfred A. Knopf, New York, 1973.

Daniels, Robert V., *The Conscience of the Revolution: Communist Opposition in Soviet Russia*, Simon & Schuster, New York, 1960.

Fitzpatrick, Sheila, *Education and Social Mobility in the Soviet Union, 1921–1934*, Cambridge University Press, Cambridge, 1979.

Fitzpatrick, Sheila, *The Cultural Front: Power and Culture in Revolutionary Russia*, Cornell University Press, Ithaca, 1992.

Kotkin, Stephen, *Stalin*, Vol. I, *Paradoxes of Power, 1878–1928*, Allen Lane, New York, 2014.

Martin, Terry, *The Affirmative Action Empire: Nations and Nationalism in the Soviet Union, 1923–1939*, Cornell University Press, Ithaca, 2001.

Rigby, T.H., *Lenin's Government: Sovnarkom 1917–1922*, Cambridge University Press, Cambridge, 1979.

Service, Robert, *Lenin: A Biography*, Harvard University Press, Cambridge, MA, 2000.

CHAPTER 3

Conquest, Robert, *The Great Terror: Stalin's Purge of the Thirties*, Macmillan, London, 1968.

Edele, Mark, *Stalinist Society, 1928–1953*, Oxford University Press, Oxford, 2011.

Fitzpatrick, Sheila (ed.), *Cultural Revolution in Russia, 1928–1931*, Indiana University Press, Bloomington, 1978.

Fitzpatrick, Sheila, *Stalin's Peasants: Resistance and Survival in the Russian Village after Collectivization*, Oxford University Press, New York, 1994.

Fitzpatrick, Sheila, *Everyday Stalinism: Ordinary Life in Extraordinary Times: Soviet Russia in the 1930s*, Oxford University Press, New York, 1999.

Getty, J. Arch and Oleg V. Naumov, *The Road to Terror: Stalin and the Self-Destruction of the Bolsheviks, 1932–1939*, Yale University Press, New Haven, 1999.

Kotkin, Stephen, *Magnetic Mountain. Stalinism as a Civilization*, University of California Press, Berkeley, 1995.

Kotkin, Stephen, *Stalin*, Vol. II, *Waiting for Hitler*, Allen Lane, New York, 2017.

Solzhenitsyn, Aleksandr I., *The Gulag Archipelago, 1918–1956*, trans. Thomas P. Whitney, Harper & Row, New York, 1973.

Viola, Lynne, *The Unknown Gulag: The Lost World of Stalin's Special Settlements*, Oxford University Press, New York, 2007.

CHAPTER 4

Alexopoulos, Golfo, 'Portrait of a Con Artist as a Soviet Man', *Slavic Review*, vol. 57, no. 4, 1998.

Bialer, Seweryn, *Stalin and His Generals: Soviet Military Memoirs of World War II*, Westview Press, Boulder, 1984.

Dunham, Vera S., *In Stalin's Time: Middle-Class Values in Soviet Fiction*, Cambridge University Press, Cambridge, 1976.

Fitzpatrick, Sheila, *On Stalin's Team: The Years of Living Dangerously in Soviet Politics*, Princeton University Press, Princeton, 2015 (see especially Chapter 9 on post-Stalin 'collective leadership').

Fitzpatrick, Sheila, 'Annexation, Evacuation and Antisemitism in the Soviet Union, 1939–1946', in Mark Edele, Sheila Fitzpatrick and Atina Grossmann (eds), *Shelter from the Holocaust: Rethinking Jewish Survival in the Soviet Union*, Wayne State University Press, Detroit, 2017.

Gorlizki, Yoram and Oleg Khlevniuk, *Cold Peace: Stalin and the Ruling Circle, 1945–1953*, Oxford University Press, Oxford, 2004.

Hessler, Julie, 'A Postwar Perestroika? Toward a History of Private Enterprise in the USSR', *Slavic Review*, vol. 57, no. 3, 1998, pp. 516–42.

Khrushchev, Nikita, *Khrushchev Remembers*, ed. and trans. Strobe Talbott, Little Brown, Boston, 1970.

Overy, Richard, *Russia's War: A History of the Soviet War Effort, 1941–1945*, Penguin, London, 1998.

Zubkova, Elena, *Russia after the War: Hopes, Illusions, and Disappointments*, ed. and trans. Hugh Ragsdale, M.E. Sharpe, Armonk, 1998.

Zubok, Vladislav, *Zhivago's Children: The Last Russian Intelligentsia*, Harvard University Press, Cambridge, MA, 2009.

CHAPTER 5

Bialer, Seweryn, *Stalin's Successors: Leadership, Stability, and Change in the Soviet Union*, Cambridge University Press, Cambridge, 1980.

Crankshaw, Edward, *Khrushchev's Russia*, Penguin, Harmondsworth, 1959.

Fitzpatrick, Sheila, 'Popular Sedition in the Post-Stalin Soviet Union', in Vladimir A. Kozlov, Sheila Fitzpatrick and Sergei V. Mironenko (eds), *Sedition: Everyday Resistance in the Soviet Union under Khrushchev and Brezhnev*, Yale University Press, New Haven, 2011.

Kozlov, Denis and Eleonory Gilburd (eds), *The Thaw: Soviet Society and Culture during the 1950s and 1960s*, University of Toronto Press, Toronto, 2013.

Ryan, Michael (comp.), *Contemporary Soviet Society. A Statistical Handbook*, Edward Elgar, Brookfield, 1990.

Taubman, William, *Khrushchev: The Man and His Era*, W.W. Norton, New York, 2003.

Zubok, Vladislav and Constantine Pleshakov, *Inside the Kremlin's Cold War: From Stalin to Khrushchev*, Harvard University Press, Cambridge, MA, 1996.

CHAPTER 6

Fitzpatrick, Sheila, *A Spy in the Archives*, Melbourne University Press, Melbourne, 2013.

Ledeneva, Alena V., *Russia's Economy of Favours: Blat, Networking and Informal Exchange*, Cambridge University Press, Cambridge, 1998.

Millar, James R., 'The Little Deal: Brezhnev's Contribution to Acquisitive Socialism', *Slavic Review*, vol. 44, no. 2, 1985, pp. 694–706.

Schattenberg, Susanne, *Brezhnev: The Making of a Stateman*, I.B. Tauris, London, 2021.

Smith, Hedrick, *The Russians*, Ballantine Books, New York, 1976.

Yurchak, Alexei, *Everything Was Forever, Until It Was No More: The Last Soviet Generation*, Princeton University Press, Princeton, 2006.

CHAPTER 7

Gill, Graeme J. and Roger D. Markwick, *Russia's Still-Born Democracy? From Gorbachev to Yeltsin*, Oxford University Press, Oxford, 2000.

Hough, Jerry F., *Democratization and Revolution in the USSR, 1985–1991*, Brookings Institution Press, Washington, DC, 1997.

Pesman, Dale, *Russia and Soul: An Exploration*, Cornell University Press, Ithaca, 2000.

Ries, Nancy, *Russian Talk: Culture and Conversation during Perestroika*, Cornell University Press, Ithaca, 1997.

Taubman, William, *Gorbachev: His Life and Times*, Simon & Schuster, New York, 2017.

White, Stephen, *Gorbachev and After*, Cambridge University Press, Cambridge, 1992.

CONCLUSION

Derluguian, Georgi M., *Bourdieu's Secret Admirer in the Caucasus: A World System Biography*, University of Chicago Press, Chicago, 2005.

Fitzpatrick, Sheila, 'Becoming Post-Soviet', in Sheila Fitzpatrick, *Tear Off the Masks! Identity and Imposture in Twentieth-Century Russia*, Princeton University Press, Princeton, 2005.

Myers, Steven Lee, *The New Tsar: The Rise and Reign of Vladimir Putin*, Alfred A. Knopf, New York, 2015.

Pelevin, Viktor, *Homo Zapiens*, trans. Andrew Bromfield, Penguin, New York, 2006.

Putin, Vladimir, Nataliya Gevorkyan, Natalya Timakova and Andrei Kolesnikov, *First Person: An Astonishingly Frank Self-Portrait by Russia's President*, trans. Catherine A. Fitzpatrick, Public Affairs, New York, 2000.

List of Images

Index